100 Awesome Icebreakers

Easy, Proven Ways to Bring Out the Best in Your Group

Patty Hupfer Riedel

The purchase of this book entitles teachers to make copies for use in their individual classrooms only. The book, or any part of it, may not be reproduced in any form for any other purpose without prior written permission from Lorenz Educational Press. It is strictly prohibited to reproduce any part of this book for an entire school or school district, or for commercial resale.

All rights reserved. Printed in the United States of America.
Copyright © 2011, Lorenz Educational Press

ISBN 978-1-4291-2240-5

BRIDGING
the Gaps in Education™
Lorenz Educational Press

for other LEP products visit our website
www.LorenzEducationalPress.com

To Anne Hupfer Stevenson,
    my sister, role model and guide
        as I've followed in her footsteps so many times.

And to Don Larsen and Earl Reum,
    for so much inspiration and the chances to lead.

Table of Contents

Introduction	4
A Lotta Hot Air	5
Add 'Em Up	5
Alphabet Dancing	6
Back to Back/People to People	7
Balloon Questions	7
Balloon Train	8
Bird on a Perch	8
Birthdays	9
Blindfold Bowling	9
Bop 'Em	10
Boundary Breaking	10
Checkerboard Challenge	13
Colored Candy Game	14
Comic Strip Lineup	14
Count Off	15
Deck of Cards – Labeling	16
Do You Like Your Neighbor?	17
Drop a Sheet	17
Eat a Meal Together – With a Twist	18
Electricity	18
Famous People	19
Find Your Mate	19
First Impressions	20
Five Fast Fill-Ins	21
Four Corners	22
Getting Into Groups	23
Giant Egg Drop	25
Gotcha!	25
Group Juggle Toss	27
Hands Down	27
Home Sweet Home	28
Hot Beach Ball	28
How Many in Your Party?	29
How Many Squares?	29
Human Bridge	31
Human Treasure Hunt	32
I Can Find That!	32
"I Didn't Know That"	34
I Gotta Hand It to You	35
Icebergs Ahead	35
Index Card Thing	36
"It Gives Me Great Pleasure to Introduce…"	36
JOY/GIVE	38
Just Like Clockwork	38
Knots	39
Line Up	39
Lucky Thirteens	40
The Mall Game	40
Monster Walk	41
Moose, Couch Potato, Mosquito	41
Musical Chair Questions	42
Name Tag	42
Name This Tune	43
Newspaper Fashion Show	43
People Bingo	44
Personal Crest	44
Picture Proverbs	47
Pipe Dreams	48
Positive Name Exchange	49
Promise Rings	49
Punch Ball Questions	50
Rapid Juggle	50
Rock, Paper, Scissors Train	51
Rope Writing	51
Rumors	52
Sandwich Cookie Solutions	54
Send Me Your Champion	55
Sentence Structure	56
Shoes!	56
Shut Eye Drawings	57
Skittergories	58
SOS	59
Sound Off	59
Spider Web	60
Story Line	61
Story Time	61
Strength Bombardment	62
Talking Buddies	62
Teamwork – LOGOS	63
Ten Nouns	63
That's Me!	64
This Is Me	65
Twelve Squares	65
Two Truths and a Lie	68
Uncommon Denominators	68
Uniquely Me	69
Up in the Air	69
Wacky Olympics	70
Walk the Plank	73
The Wave	73
Web of Info	74
What I Like About Me Is	74
What's Different?	75
What's in a Name?	75
When Someone Claps Twice	76
Who's in Charge?	78
Wink	78
Yes/No Line	79
Yes – No – Blue – Black	80
Zip, Zap, Zoop	80

Introduction

Active Learning

I teach chemistry, and I want my students to feel comfortable enough to ask questions of me or of anyone else in the class. Chemistry is a tough subject. If you are afraid to reach out for help, you can have a pretty rough time. That is why I build in experiential, or active, learning experiences, through which group members learn by taking part in games, role playing, problem solving, debates, competitions, and communications. Icebreakers help people get to know one another, relax, laugh, and feel part of a team. This process of getting acquainted and team building is important in school groups, church groups, corporate meetings – and chemistry classes. It is necessary for all age groups.

Active Learning – in a non-threatening way – has a number of advantages:

- The time spent together in a group helps form relationships or make established relationships stronger. That's the priority.
- Students enjoy being involved. It's not "sit down, be quiet, and listen."
- It encourages creativity, and promotes thought and ideas. Group members aren't told the answers. They find the answers.
- It provides a safe place to make mistakes and learn from them.

How to Use This Book

The activities in this book are pretty straightforward. Most need no supplies, and the rest need very few. All activities have been tested, and they work. Of course, you are the best judge for deciding if a particular activity is appropriate for your class. The activities are great for a variety of group sizes, so they are perfect for clubs, extracurricular activities, retreats and youth groups, as well as for general classroom use.

The activities are arranged alphabetically by title. If there is any worksheet needed for an activity, it is provided immediately after the activity.

Read the rules of each activity more than once before using it so that you feel comfortable with it. Some activities are done just for fun, but many can be processed or discussed at the end, which is often the best part of the whole exercise. I'm continually amazed at what each group gets out of the various activities, and how the same activity can spark different reactions from different groups.

I did not set an age range for each activity. With a few adaptations, I believe they work with any age. From my own use of these activities, I know that your groups will benefit from them and I also know that you will as well. Just don't forget to bring your own enthusiasm, openness, and energy to every group gathering. Now jump in and enjoy!

A Lotta Hot Air

Purpose: Promotes teamwork while having a lot of fun
Group Size: 16 or more
Time: 10 – 15 minutes
Supplies: One straw per person; two facial tissues for each team

Directions:

1. Divide the group into two equal teams. If you have a very large number of students, break the group into teams of eight to ten players. See *Getting into Groups* on pages 23-24 for suggestions.
2. Have each team form a line.
3. Give each student a straw.
4. Explain that when you say "Go," the first person in line is to suck the tissue onto the end of the straw, and then pass it to the next person in line. That person must suck the tissue onto his or her straw and pass it to the next person in line.
5. No hands may be used. If the tissue falls to the floor, the team member who last had the tissue must suck it off the floor with his or her straw.
6. The team that gets a tissue to the end of the line first is the winner.

Add 'Em Up

Purpose: Promotes lively competition with an easy addition challenge
Group Size: 10 or more
Time: 5 minutes
Supplies: None

Directions:

1. Have everyone pair off and face each other.
2. Each person holds his or her hand in a fist. Together they count "one, two, three," and on "three" each player in the pair shoots out zero, one, two, three, four or five fingers so the other player can see it.
3. The first player to add up and shout out the total number of fingers held out is declared the winner.
4. Play the best two out of three to determine the winner of that round.
5. Have everyone change partners, introduce themselves, and repeat the exercise.

5

Alphabet Dancing

Purpose: Good exercise in healthy competition, instant cooperation and organization; works well in helping a group of strangers get to know one another
Group Size: 20 to 40
Time: 10 minutes
Supplies: Two sets of index cards with capital letters of the alphabet written on each (one letter per card, for a total of 52 cards)

Directions:

1. Divide the group into two teams.
2. Place a stack of alphabet cards on each of two chairs or tables that are set fifteen to twenty feet away from two starting lines.
3. Direct each team to stand behind one of the starting lines.
4. Have your list of words ready (see suggestions below). When you call out a word, each team must send a player for each letter of the word to the stack of cards. They must find the correct letters and hold them up in the proper order so that you can read the word. For instance, if you say CAT, three people run to the letters, grab one C, one A, and one T. Then they must arrange themselves in order, and hold up the cards so that you can read the word CAT.
5. The team who spells the word correctly first gets a point. After the word is spelled, the letters should be returned to the stack. You can play until one team has earned a designated number of points or until you've exhausted your list of words. The team that has the most points at that time wins.
6. Sometimes it's good to have two referees watching the competition, and they can rule on who completed the spelling first.
7. Suggested words to use:

dreams	goals	driveway	chemistry
outlaw	listen	quietly	laughter
New York	angels	thunder	wishful
harmonic	symbolic	rhyme	holiday

8. With just the 26 letters of the alphabet, you are limited to words with no duplicate letters. If you want to add another E, T, S, R, A or L to the set of letters, you can spell many more words.

Variation: Ask a question and each team has to spell out the answer.

Back to Back/People to People

Purpose: Gives students a high-energy game in which they interact with a large number of people
Group Size: 25 or more
Time: 15 minutes
Supplies: None

Directions:

1. Everyone must have a partner except the person who is "It." If the partners don't know each other, they should introduce themselves.
2. "It" calls out directions such as "back to back," "shoulder to shoulder," "foot to knee," "hand to head," "head to head," and so on.
3. Partners must position their bodies in the manner directed by "It."
4. When "It" calls out "People to People," everyone – including "It" – must find a new partner.
5. The one person left without a partner is the new "It," who then calls out a new set of directions.
6. Make sure "It" keeps the directions flowing in order to give the game a high-energy pace.
7. When partners change, remind them to introduce themselves if they don't know each other.

Balloon Questions

Purpose: An interactive getting-to-know-you activity
Group Size: 10 to 30
Time: 15 – 30 minutes
Supplies: One balloon for each person; questions written on small strips of paper, one tucked inside each balloon (for starters, see suggested *Boundary-Breaking Questions* on pages 11 and 12)

Directions:

1. Give each person a non-inflated balloon with a question rolled up and tucked inside. Balloons need not be inflated to save you time, but if you want to inflate them beforehand, that's ok, too.
2. Have students blow up their balloons and tie them shut.
3. On the count of three, everyone tosses the balloons into the air. The group has to keep all balloons in the air for one minute in order to mix up the balloons. This also gives the group something active to do before they sit down to answer the questions.
4. When you say "Stop," everyone should grab a balloon and hold onto it.
5. Ask for a volunteer. Instruct the volunteer to pick someone to help pop his or her balloon.
6. After the balloon is popped, the person reads the question and answers it aloud. The person who helped pop the balloon goes next, choosing someone else to assist him or her.
7. Having someone help pop the balloon keeps a flow to the order of the activity. Another advantage to having a helper is that some people don't like popping balloons, and it's nice to have moral support.

Balloon Train

Purpose: A team activity that requires a lot of cooperation among members
Group Size: Unlimited, divided into teams of 8 to 10
Time: 10 minutes
Supplies: Large balloon for each person; one chair or cone for each team

Directions:

1. Divide the group into teams of eight to ten (see *Getting into Groups* on pages 23-24 for suggestions). Each team should form a single-file line behind a starting point. Have a chair or cone about 30 feet away from each starting line to serve as the turn-around point.
2. Ask each person, except the head of the line, to blow up a balloon.
3. One balloon is placed between each person on the team, so the members must be close enough to one another to keep the balloons from falling to the ground.
4. The object of the game is to see which team can go from the starting point, around the chair or cone, and back to the starting point the fastest without losing any balloons.

Variation: Make the course more of an obstacle course by arranging things in the way of the team members. They may have to go over chairs, under branches, around objects, or through narrow spaces.

Bird on a Perch

Purpose: Provides a fast-action competition that is a lot of fun
Group Size: 20 to 100
Time: 15 minutes
Supplies: Music (radio, CD player or MP3 player)

Directions:

1. Have each player find a partner.
2. Form an inner and outer circle with one partner in the inner circle and one partner in the outer circle. The partners should stand facing each other.
3. When the music starts, the inner circle begins to move clockwise and the outer circle moves counter-clockwise. When the music stops, the partners must run to each other. One partner gets down on one knee and the other partner sits on that knee. Then they must freeze.
4. The last set of partners to get down on one knee is out of the game. Any other pair that moves – doesn't stay frozen – until the music starts again, is also out of the game.
5. Play until only one pair is left.

Birthdays

Purpose: Divides a large group into smaller groups while discovering some common ground among group members
Group Size: Unlimited (the bigger the better)
Time: 15 – 30 minutes
Supplies: None

Directions:

1. Tell everyone to find all the other people who have the same birth month. (It can get loud at this point!)
2. When it seems that most people have found their groups, call out "Where is the group with the January birthdays?" (Continue with each month of the year until you have all of the months that are represented.) Do this to make sure that all groups are together and not fragmented.
3. Instruct each group to make up a cheer, poem, or song (15 to 30 seconds long) that represents their birth month. Allow no more than five minutes for this.
4. Have each group present the results of their teamwork.

Blindfold Bowling

Purpose: To learn teamwork and communication
Group Size: 10 to 20
Time: 15 – 30 minutes
Supplies: Plastic bowling balls and pins; blindfolds

Directions:

1. Divide the group into two teams.
2. Set up the pins as you would in a normal bowling game, about 25 to 30 feet away from the bowler.
3. Blindfold the first bowler and spin him or her around seven times.
4. The people on that bowler's team can give directions so the bowler will be in the vicinity of the pins, but they cannot touch the bowler. The bowler must throw the bowling ball before 15 seconds elapse.
5. Keep a record of the number of pins knocked down after each player tosses the ball one time. If pins were knocked down, reset them before the next bowler's turn.
6. Alternate bowlers between the two teams. The winning team is the one with the highest score.
7. Discuss how each team communicated with its blindfold bowler and how that helped or hindered his or her bowling ability.

Bop 'Em

Purpose: Gets everyone involved, a particularly good energizer between long listening sessions
Group Size: Unlimited, divided into groups of 5 to 7
Time: 5 minutes
Supplies: 2 balloons for each group

Directions:

1. Divide any large group into smaller groups of five to seven people (see *Getting into Groups* on pages 23-24 for suggestions).
2. Blow up one balloon for each group. (The second can be used as a reserve if the first one pops, or you can add it to the game if you want to make it more difficult.)
3. Each group holds hands and sees how long they can keep the balloon in the air by only using their heads and elbows to keep it up. Have them count the number of times it is hit legally.
4. Next have the groups use only their feet and knees. Again, have them count the number of times it stays in the air legally.
5. Lastly, have the groups try their knees and their hands that are still clasped together.

Boundary Breaking

Purpose: Provides a quiet listening activity in which group members learn about one another by paying attention to tone of voice and body language
Group Size: 10 to 30
Time: 1 – 2 hours
Supplies: List of questions

Directions:

1. Set the atmosphere by dimming the lights in the room if possible.
2. Sit around a large table or in a circle. No one should be left out of the group, and the circle is to be as tight as possible.
3. Read a question and invite the person to your left to answer the question first. Continue around the circle until everyone has answered. You should be answering the questions yourself as your turn comes. There should be no debate about any answer nor should any further questions be asked. It is strictly a time to listen and learn.
4. Each person should answer every question. Members may initially "pass" on a question, but you should always come back to them at a later time to answer it.
5. When you ask the second question, invite the second person from your left to answer first. Continue to move one person to the left for each subsequent question.
6. Try to ask as many questions as your time frame allows without rushing anyone's answer.

Boundary-Breaking Questions

1. What are you most looking forward to in the next three months?
2. For what one thing do you want to be remembered?
3. What is one talent you would like to possess?
4. What article of clothing that your mom or dad wears embarrasses you the most?
5. What is your greatest accomplishment?
6. If you had a crystal ball and could see the future, what one thing would you want to find out?
7. What is one of your pet peeves?
8. What one thing do you hope to accomplish in school?
9. Share something about your family that makes you proud.
10. If you could travel to any place in time, when and where would you go?
11. What is the best movie you have ever seen?
12. What's the best concert you've ever seen?
13. What do you want to be doing ten years from now?
14. Finish this statement: "The best thing about today is…."
15. What kind of store would you like to own and operate?
16. If you could have dinner with anyone, living or dead, who would it be?
17. What person has most influenced your life?
18. What is the best compliment you have received?
19. If you could travel to any place in the world, where would you go first?
20. What future discovery are you most looking forward to?
21. Share three things for which you are thankful.
22. Select a word that best describes your life at this time.
23. What would you like to invent to make life easier?
24. Tell about the greatest present you have ever given or received.
25. What emotion is strongest in you?
26. What makes you laugh?
27. How do you like to spend your free time?
28. In your opinion, what profession benefits society most?
29. Share a goal you have set and reached.
30. What makes a house a home?
31. If you could change your age, how old would you be?
32. If you had three wishes, what would they be?
33. What is the best / last book you have read?
34. What is your favorite television program?
35. Describe your room.
36. What is your favorite holiday?
37. Do you think the world will be a better or worse place 100 years from now?
38. If each day had six more hours, how would you spend them?
39. What would constitute a perfect evening for you?
40. Would you rather receive $10,000 for yourself or $100,000 to give away?
41. What is your favorite quote?
42. What subject is most frequently discussed among your friends?
43. What one day in your life would you like to relive?
44. What is your least favorite TV commercial?
45. What event in your life has been a turning point for you?

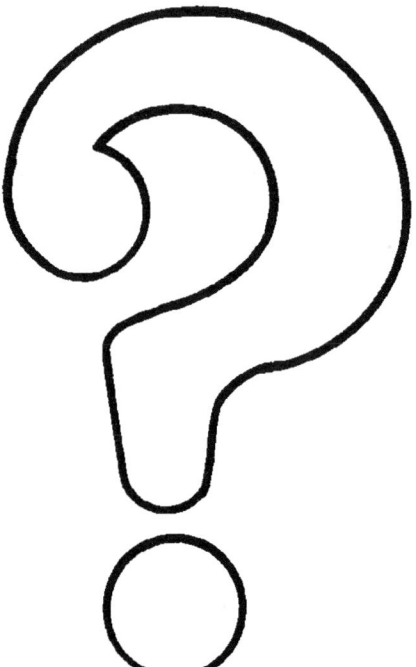

Boundary-Breaking Questions, cont'd.

46. Besides your parents, who do you most admire?
47. If you were going to write a TV show about yourself, what type would you write – soap opera, comedy, romance, drama? Why?
48. Do you believe in miracles?
49. What one characteristic do you see in yourself that you also see in your parents/grandparents?
50. In your opinion, what is the most pressing problem in the world today?
51. When you feel sad or angry, what do you do to express yourself? How do you cheer yourself back up?
52. What is your favorite way to spend an evening with your parents?
53. Of the five senses – sight, smell, touch, taste or hearing – which could you live without? Which could you not bear to lose?
54. How important is money to you?
55. Would you tell the truth no matter what? When would you ever lie?
56. If you were a fly on the wall, on whom would you want to eavesdrop?
57. What one thing would you place in a time capsule that would be discovered by future generations?
58. What is your passion/purpose in life?
59. If your house was burning (and all of your loved ones and pets were safe), what three possessions would you save?
60. If you could offer one piece of advice to your parents, what would it be?
61. What day are you most looking forward to?
62. What is the most beautiful thing you have ever seen?
63. When do you feel most productive?
64. Finish this sentence: "I hope..."
65. Describe your best phone call ever.
66. If you could trade places with someone, who would it be?
67. What, if anything, is too serious to be joked about?
68. Describe your feelings about_____(yourself, love, religion, music, the news)
69. Do you consider yourself a leader? Why or why not?
70. When do you feel most lonely?
71. Describe the person with whom you would like to spend the rest of your life.
72. What is the most stressful event you've ever experienced?
73. What do you think people like about you the most/least?
74. What is your most treasured memory?
75. What is your most important goal now?
76. What should you do that you have put off?
77. What is the best song you've ever heard?
78. What is the best thing about your home town?
79. In summer, what do you like to do?
80. With whom would you like to co-star in a movie?
81. What concert would you like to attend?
82. What would you do with an hour of free time?
83. If you could interview anyone, whom would you choose?
84. Describe your best friend.
85. How did you feel about your last haircut?
86. What is one of your bad habits?
87. If you could be any cartoon character, which would you be?
88. When was the last time you laughed out loud? At what?
89. What do you miss the most about your childhood?
90. Is there anything else you would like the group to know about you?

Checkerboard Challenge

Purpose: Encourages problem solving, team communication and strategizing

Group Size: 6 to 12

Time: 10 minutes, plus discussion

Supplies: Masking tape to make the checkerboard on the floor, or a checkerboard pattern taped on a tarp that can be used again

Directions:

1. Tape the checkerboard pattern to the floor and show it to the group. Tell them that there is a secret path that enables them to cross the checkerboard. The problem is that only you know the secret path. Students have to find the path by trial and error. The choices for correct squares will always be forward, diagonally forward, or sideways.
2. No one can talk or communicate in any way once the game begins, so some planning within the group has to take place ahead of time. Allow a few minutes for strategizing and for the team to decide in what order each member will go.
3. Only one person can be on the board at a time, and each player must have a turn before anyone tries a second time.
4. The first person in line steps on a square. If it is an incorrect square, you "buzz" the move and the player goes to the end of the line. If it is the correct square, the player may try another square.
5. As each player's turn comes, he or she should know which squares have been buzzed and which haven't.
6. A player's turn continues until he or she steps on an incorrect square. The object is to get the whole team across the board using the correct squares.
7. You should have a few patterns already drawn out that you will allow the group to follow. A couple of samples are below, but you can work out others as needed.

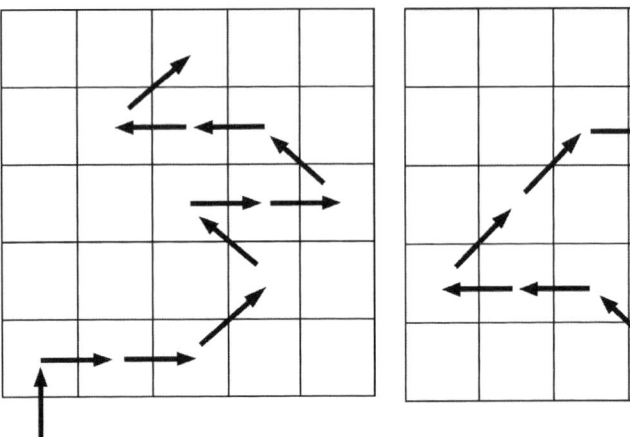

8. After the game is ended, process the activity:

    - Share stories about the game.
    - What was frustrating about the rules, and why?
    - What was good about the rules, and why?
    - If you could play again, would you change anything?
    - What is important about choosing the right strategy?
    - How could you relate what you learned to real-life problems?

Colored Candy Game

Purpose: Provides a fun (and tasty) way to get to know others
Group Size: 5 to 20
Time: 20 – 40 minutes
Supplies: One fun-size pack of colored chocolate candy for every group member (make sure to check that no one has a food allergy)

Directions:

1. Arrange group members in a circle and give each person a fun-size pack of candies.
2. Each person should open his or her pack and group the candies by color. Each color of candy represents a different topic. The following categories are just suggestions. Make up categories that fit your group, or if you would prefer, ask more specific questions. Adjust the colors for the candy you use.

Red	hobbies you have or would like to have
Blue	things about your family that they wouldn't mind you sharing
Yellow	things about yourself that you are proud of
Green	places to which you've traveled
Brown	things you'd like to do in the next ten years
Orange	goals for yourself this year

3. The number of candies of a certain color a player has determines the number of responses they have to share with the group. For instance, if Player A has three red candies, he or she should name three hobbies. If Player B has one red candy, he or she names one hobby.
4. Have everyone respond to the same color as you take turns around the circle. When all the reds have been answered, then move on to the next color.
5. Don't forget to eat the candy as you go along!

Comic Strip Lineup

Purpose: Helps split a large group into smaller groups; encourages working together to solve a problem
Group Size: 15 to 100
Time: 10 minutes
Supplies: Comic strips cut into single panels; masking tape

Directions:

1. Give each group member a comic strip panel and a piece of masking tape. Have members tape their panels to their shirt fronts.
2. Have everyone walk around and find others who have parts of the same comic strip.
3. Once they all find one another, group members should arrange themselves in the correct order for the comic strip to make sense.
4. When all groups are finished, have each completed group come to the front of the room, identify themselves by the comic strip they represent, and read the strips aloud.

Count Off

Purpose: A problem-solving activity; an energizer that gets the group working together
Group Size: 10 to 40
Time: 5 – 10 minutes
Supplies: None

Directions:

1. Students should be positioned randomly around the room.
2. Tell the group to count from 1 to 21. This sounds easy, but students must follow these guidelines:

   - Only one person may say a number at a time.
   - No one person may say two or more consecutive numbers.
   - The numbers must be said in sequence.
   - If more than one person says a number at the same time, the group must start over.
   - No other talking may occur once the counting begins.

3. When you say "Go," the counting begins.
4. If the group is really having trouble, stop the game and tell the students that they can make up one rule. It's interesting to see how that can speed the game along.
5. After finishing, process the activity with the following questions:

   - Was this a tough task? Why or why not?
   - How did you establish a pattern?
   - What verbal and non-verbal clues did you use to know who would go next?
   - What would make your task easier?
   - How can you relate this to habits of communication?

Deck of Cards – Labeling

Purpose: Demonstrates how we label people before really getting to know one another
Group Size: 15 to 50
Time: 10 minutes
Supplies: Deck of cards

Directions:

1. Give everyone in the group a card, and tell students NOT to look at it.
2. After the cards have been distributed, tell students to hold their cards on their forehead so that the other group members can see it.
3. Everyone should then mingle around the room and react to people according to the following standards:

    - People with Aces, Kings, Queens or Jacks should be treated with the most respect. These are the people you want to get to know. Seek them out.
    - Those with Twos, Threes or Fours should be avoided at all costs.
    - Those who hold cards Five through Ten should be treated at an appropriate level according to their number; that is, they should be spoken to, but not in depth or for very long.

4. Let the group mingle for about two minutes, and then have everyone guess their cards. Then students may look at their cards.
5. Process the activity with these or other questions of your own:

    - What card did you think you had on your forehead?
    - In what ways did others in the group react to you?
    - How did those with low cards feel during this activity?
    - How did those with high cards feel during this activity?
    - What kind of things do we notice when we label people?

6. After processing the activity, stress that we need to treat one another as "high cards" if we truly want to make a difference.

Do You Like Your Neighbor?

Purpose: Provides practice in remembering names while learning more about other group members
Group Size: 15 to 30
Time: 15 – 20 minutes
Supplies: One sturdy chair for each student except the group leader

Directions:

1. Everyone should sit in a circle with the leader in the center.
2. The leader steps in front of one of the group members and asks "[Name], do you like your neighbor?"
3. The responding person, using the names of the people on his or her left and right, says, "Yes, I like my neighbors [Name] and [Name]." Continuing, the responder says, "But I really like people who…." The responder should complete the sentence with something that will describe others in the group. For instance:
   … who have birthdays in summer.
   … saw "The Lion King."
4. Anyone who fits into the category mentioned must stand up and trade places with others who fit into the same category. During the exchange, the leader tries to get a seat. The person left standing is the new leader.
5. If you like, another rule can be added. The leader asks the question, "Do you like your neighbor?" The person asked can respond "Switch!" At that point, all group members must change places.
6. Game continues for as long as desired.

Drop a Sheet

Purpose: Helps people learn the names of students; explores reactions to being "on the spot"
Group Size: 15 to 30
Time: 10 minutes
Supplies: Sheet, blanket or tarp (something you can't see through)

Directions:

1. Divide the group into two even teams. You also need two sheet holders (you can be one of them if you wish).
2. The sheet, which will serve as the wall, is held up as high as possible while still touching the floor.
3. Teams sit on either side of the sheet so that they cannot see each other.
4. Each group secretly selects one person to walk up to within a foot of the sheet. On the count of three, the sheet holders lower the sheet.
5. The first of the two people at the sheet to shout out the other's name correctly wins that round and gets a point for his or her team.
6. Continue the process with two new people at the sheet. The winning team is the one with the most points at the end of the game.
7. Process the activity by asking:
   - Why might you want or not want to face another when the sheet is dropped?
   - What makes this game easy? What makes this game difficult?
   - What does pressure do to your focus?

Note: Watch out for windows, mirrors or TV screens that might reflect and show the other side of the sheet.

Eat a Meal Together – With a Twist

Purpose: Helps form a bond within the group; encourages members to really take notice of those around them

Group Size: 6 to 15

Time: 30 – 60 minutes (more if you include cleanup)

Supplies: Food and utensils needed for your meal; string

Directions:

1. Tell the group ahead of time that they are going to be eating a meal together. The meal could be pizza, spaghetti, hotdogs or anything you like, but it should not all be on their plate when they arrive. You want the group to do as much for themselves as possible to get the meal together.
2. After everyone is assembled and before you begin the meal, tie each person's wrist to the next person's wrist with a short string. This should make it so that if one person's hand moves, the person next to him or her has to move, too.
3. Things such as passing the ketchup or using a fork have to be negotiated between the people tied together.
4. If you'd like, have the students clean the table and do the dishes while still connected.
5. Discuss how the group worked together and how they really had to be conscious of one another. Share funny stories about the adventure.

Electricity

Purpose: Gets everyone involved in a fun exercise of teamwork and competition

Group Size: 16 to 40

Time: 10 – 20 minutes

Supplies: Coin; object to grab at the end of the line

Directions:

1. Form the group into two even lines, with each person in line facing a member of the other team. Decide which end of the line is the head. The person at the head of the line is the line leader for the first round.
2. Place an object to be picked up at the end of the line, equidistant from the last people in the two lines (they will be the "grabbers"). There should be only one object for the two lines. Some objects you might use include a stuffed animal, a roll of tape or a ball of yarn.
3. Instruct all teammates to hold hands, and all except the line leaders should close their eyes.
4. The leaders should keep their eyes on you as you flip a coin. Hold up the coin to allow the leaders to see whether it landed on heads or tails.
5. If it is heads, each line leader squeezes the hand he or she is holding. The squeeze should be passed down the line as quickly as possible. When the last person feels the squeeze, he or she should grab the object at the end of the line and hold it up. The team with the object is awarded one point.
6. If it is tails, no squeeze should be started. If one of the line leaders mistakenly starts the squeeze and it reaches the end of the line, the team loses one point. If no one squeezes, you'll know after a few seconds by the lack of reaction. Then go on to the next coin toss.
7. Once the line leaders have had a chance to squeeze hands (after the first toss that lands heads), they go to the end of the line. Now the next two people become the line leaders. The game continues in the same way.

Famous People

Purpose: Gives students a fun, relaxed way of mixing without having to reveal personal information
Group Size: 10 to 50
Time: 10 minutes
Supplies: Adhesive nametag for each student, or make nametags from slips of paper with a loop of tape on one side

Directions:

1. On each nametag or slip of paper, write the name of a famous person (living or dead).
2. Attach a nametag to each person's back.
3. Each group member has to figure out whose name is on his or her back by asking other students only questions that can be answered "yes" or "no." ("Is this person a female/male?" "Is she in the entertainment business?" "Was he famous in the 90s?" "Did she ever do voices with cartoon characters?")
4. Play until everyone has figured out the name of the famous person on their backs.

Find Your Mate

Purpose: Helps form pairs out of a large group; provides practice in solving problems
Group Size: Unlimited
Time: 10 minutes
Supplies: An index card or small sheet of paper for each student containing the name of half of a famous pair (see examples below); strips of adhesive or masking tape

Directions:

1. Tape a card or paper to each person's back.
2. Explain that everyone must first figure out what or who is written on their back, and that they must then find the other half of the pair.
3. Students must limit their questions to those that can be answered "yes" or "no," and they can ask only three questions of the same person. After three questions are asked, they must move on to other people.
4. Continue with the game until everyone is paired up.
5. At this point, you can conclude the activity or begin another activity that requires paired students.

Variation: A quick change in this activity is to have everyone wear their index cards on their front sides. This way they know what or who they are and can just look for their partners. This works faster and is especially good for younger people or very large groups.

<u>Sample Pairs</u>
peanut butter/jelly
macaroni/cheese
chocolate/vanilla
pen/pencil
police officer/criminal
teacher/student
peas/carrots
black/white
chair/table

First Impressions

Purpose: Highlights the impact of first impressions and how different people have different impressions of the same person, incident, or situation

Group Size: 5 to 50

Time: 15 – 20 minutes

Supplies: 4 or more pictures of people in various situations, dress, or habitats; pencil and paper for each student

Directions:

1. Distribute paper and pencils.
2. Hold up one of the pictures, and ask the students to write down their first impression of the person in the picture. Give examples to get the group started if you think they need some ideas. For example, ask, "Is this person happy? Rich? Nice? Does he or she have a job? Would you like to be this person's friend? What do you think this person's hobbies are? Where is this person from?"
3. Hold up the next picture. Again, have students write down their first impressions of the person in the picture.
4. Do the same for a third and fourth picture.
5. Return to the first picture and ask the students to share some of the ideas they wrote down. Do the same with the other pictures.
6. Process the activity:

   - Why did you write some of the things you did?
   - What gave you those impressions? (Do each picture separately.)
   - How do we judge one another? What characteristics do we look for?
   - Have you ever had a first impression of someone that later changed because you got to know that person? Explain.
   - What kind of impression do you think others have of you?
   - Is a first impression important?
   - How do you make a good first impression?
   - What can you do this week to change the way you judge people?

Five Fast Fill-Ins

Purpose: Use as quick lessons, energizers, or for short breaks
Group Size: Unlimited
Time: 5 minutes or less
Supplies: Paper; pen or pencil

Attitude

Have everyone write out the word ATTITUDE on a piece of paper. Assign a number value to each letter of the alphabet: A=1, B=2, C=3, D=4 and so on. Once the letter values are assigned, have students add the totals for the word ATTITUDE (it should add up to 100). Discuss how everything you do in life comes down to your attitude about it. Having a positive attitude will help you get 100% out of life.

N or M States?

Ask the group to quickly get into smaller groups of two or three (see *Getting into Groups* on pages 23-24 for suggestions). Tell students that you are going to give them one minute to figure out the answer to this question: Are there more states that start with the letter M or the letter N? After one minute, ask for a show of hands from those who think there are more states that begin with the letter M. Then do the same for the letter N. They may be surprised to learn that there are eight states that begin with each of these letters. See if the groups can name all 16 states.

20 Words in 20 Seconds

Have the group get in smaller groups of three. Ask the groups to think of 20 words in 20 seconds that do not have the letter A in them. It's fun to see what the groups can come up with in that short amount of time. It seems that when you mention the letter A, you can't help but focus on the letter A, and this simple exercise becomes difficult.

Hand Clasp – Habits

Tell everyone to stretch their arms out in front of them. Then ask students to clasp their hands together, with fingers interlocking. Tell them to look at which thumb is on the top: is it the left or right thumb? Now have students change their grip so that the opposite thumb is on the top. How does that feel? Usually, it feels very strange and unfamiliar.
The lesson here is that change is often very uncomfortable. But if you clasped your hands the opposite (uncomfortable) way every day for 21 days, it would start to feel "normal," because new habits take this long to establish. Point out how helpful this can be when trying to acquire good habits.

Variation: Do the same exercise with crossing your arms. It's harder and funnier to watch.

What Color Is This?

Hold up a white piece of paper and ask the group, "What color is this?" They will answer, "White." Ask again, "What color is this?" They again should say, "White." Ask two more times, each time getting the answer "white." Finally ask, "What do cows drink?" Most of the group will say, "Milk." They'll know you got them because they will realize the answer should have been "water." Use this just for fun or to talk about how easily we can get thrown off the right track by diversions.

Variation: Ask a group this series of questions:
1. What do bunnies do to move? ("Hop")
2. What is on a long stick and used for cleaning? ("Mop")
3. What is another word for Dad? ("Pop")
4. The opposite of bottom is ___. ("Top")
5. What do you do at a green light? ("Go") Most will answer "Stop."

Four Corners

Purpose: Provides a simple game of grouping and regrouping that also reveals a lot about the students; self-assessments
Group Size: 10 to 30
Time: 15 – 30 minutes
Supplies: None

Directions:

1. Have the group assemble in the middle of the room and remain standing.
2. Explain that you will be calling out a variety of categories, and that each student will need to decide in which category he or she belongs.
3. Explain that as you call out the categories, you will point to a specific corner of the room for each of the choices. Students are to go to whatever corner they think "fits" them.
4. Begin by saying to the group, "Are you more like…" and fill in the blank with one of the following options:

    - 6 A.M., noon, 6 P.M., midnight
    - fire truck, pickup truck, school bus, Ferrari
    - chef salad, hamburger and fries, spaghetti, filet mignon
    - English, social studies, art, science
    - golf club, catcher's mask, swim goggles, bowling bag
    - western, comedy, romance, thriller
    - merry-go-round, swings, slide, monkey bars
    - Hawaii, Colorado, Washington DC, Las Vegas
    - giraffe, tiger, parrot, elephant

5. After you finish each category and all group members are in their corners, go around the room quickly and let people share a few of the reasons they chose that group. (There is often great insight and wisdom put into their choices!)
6. When that step is completed, pick another category and begin again.
7. When you are finished with the categories, process the activity if you feel more discussion is helpful:

    - What did you learn about the reasons people chose their corners?
    - Were you with different people every time? Why do you think that is?
    - What were some of the most unique reasons people had for choosing a group?
    - What did you learn about other group members from this activity?

Getting Into Groups

Purpose: Provides creative options for getting into groups

Pairing Up

- Everyone holds up either a thumb or pinky. All should quickly find someone with the same thing in the air.
- Everyone stands on one foot. Find a partner who is on the opposite foot.
- Everyone secretly picks a vacation spot (give two choices, like the Bahamas or Colorado; Disney World or Sea World). Pair up with someone who is going to the same place.
- Pair up with the first person you meet who is wearing a shirt that is the same (or similar) color as your shirt.
- Make the sound of a cat or a dog. Pair up with the first person you hear making the same sound.
- Call out "chocolate" or "vanilla." Pair up with someone who chose a different flavor.

Using a Deck of Cards (Deal one card to each student.)

- Get together with all people holding a card of the same number (groups of four).
- Get together with those holding a card of the same suit (groups of 13 or less.) **Note**: You control the number of each suit in the deck according to how many groups you want.
- Find the best poker hand (group of five).
- Find a pair (group of two).
- Find one card of each suit (group of four).

Animal Noises

As people arrive, give each student a slip with an animal's name on it, or whisper it in their ear. Use as many different animals as you need teams. Tell everyone to close their eyes and make the animal sound. Students must try to find the others in their group just by following the sounds.

Nametags

Put a colored dot or identifying sticker on each nametag before the gathering starts. (If you need five groups, use five distinctive dots or stickers.) When you are ready to break into groups, tell each person to check his or her nametag and find the others who belong to the same group.

Humdingers

Determine how many teams you need. Give each player a strip of paper that has a childhood song on it, or you can whisper the name of the song in each person's ear. Some examples are "Happy Birthday," "Mary Had a Little Lamb," "Row, Row, Row Your Boat," and "Twinkle, Twinkle Little Star." Everyone hums their song and forms a group with all people humming the same song.

Getting Into Groups, cont'd.

Phone Number

Tell the group to pretend that the classroom is the keypad of a touchtone phone. They need to think of the last digit of their phone number and go to the space in the room that would correspond to that number on the keypad. (You will most likely end up with uneven group sizes.)

Puzzlers

Cut several large pictures out of magazines. Make sure each picture is distinctly different from the others. Cut each picture into as many pieces as you need members in each group. Mix up all the pieces and have each person draw one out of a bag. The challenge is to find others with pieces from the same picture. When they find each other, they put the picture back together.

Clipped Together

Decide how many groups you need, and use that many different colors of paper clips. Mix all the clips together. Have all students pick a clip and find all others that have the same color. They should then make a long paper clip chain with their group members.

Seasons

Have everyone count off by saying "spring," "summer," "fall," and "winter." To form four groups, everyone from each season should get together. To form a group of four people, one person from each season should get together.

Whatevers

Determine how many teams you want – this is the number of categories you need. For instance, if you need two teams, have everyone find a partner and decide between them who wants to be an apple and who wants to be an orange (or sun/moon; refrigerator/freezer; 100/200). Once they've decided, tell all the apples to get on one side and all the oranges to go to the other side. If you want three teams, you could use sun/moon/stars or rock/paper/scissors. For four teams you could use spring/summer/fall/winter, and so on.

Giant Egg Drop

Purpose: Highlights creativity in team work
Group Size: 10 to 15, divided into teams of 4 or 5
Time: 20 – 30 minutes
Supplies: Fill a paper lunch bag with the following items for each team: 2 tongue depressors, 4 rubber bands, 1 paper cup, 1 sheet of newspaper, 10 toothpicks, 1 foot of masking tape, 1 raw egg

Directions:

1. Divide the group into teams of four or five (see *Getting into Groups* on pages 23-24 for suggestions).
2. Give each group a bag of supplies.
3. Tell the teams that they have 15 minutes to construct something that will help their egg survive a two-story drop.
4. After time is up, allow each group to show off their design.
5. Discuss which design everyone thinks will work the best.
6. Test each design by dropping it out of a two-story building or from a 15-foot height onto a hard surface. A tall ladder will also work.
7. Process the activity:

   - Whose design worked the best? Was it the same one you predicted?
   - How did you feel about your group's design after it was completed?
   - How did you go about designing your egg protector? Were ideas from all team members used, or was just one person's idea used?
   - Did you give all of your input, or did you hold back some of your ideas from the group? When have you done that in other times of your life?
   - Did you believe your group's idea would work? Why or why not?
   - What did you learn from this activity?

Gotcha!

Purpose: Establishes a fun structure for meeting others; good activity for learning names plus a little additional information
Group Size: 25 or more (the more the better!)
Time: 10 minutes
Supplies: Gotcha! Worksheet for each student; pen or pencil for each student

Directions:

1. Everyone should have a copy of the Gotcha! Worksheet (page 26) and a pen or pencil.
2. Each person has ten minutes to accomplish everything on the sheet and to get the required signatures.

Gotcha! Worksheet

Do everything on this list, and get signatures to prove it. No duplicate signatures please!

1. Untie someone's shoe, and then tie it again. Have the person sign here:
   _____

2. Count out loud (as loud as you can) as you do ten jumping jacks with a partner. Have your partner sign here:
   _____

3. Find someone who is left-handed. Have them sign their name using their RIGHT hand.
   _____

4. Have someone else do five push-ups for you. Have this person sign here:
   _____

5. Get someone to sing a TV commercial and sign here:
   _____

6. Do your very best impersonation of a cow, pig or chicken for someone, and have them sign here:
   _____

7. Find someone whose birthday is the same month as yours, and ask the person to sign both his or her name and month of birth:

   Name _____

   Birth Month _____

8. Have six people sign their names and places of birth on the back of this sheet.

9. Find someone whose eyes are a different color from yours and have them sign here:
   _____

10. Get four other people to form a circle with you and sing one verse of "Row, Row, Row Your Boat." Have the four people sign the back of this sheet.
    _____

11. Ask someone to let you borrow a coin and to sign here:
    _____

12. Find six people and have a group hug! Have them put their initials in the box: ☐

Group Juggle Toss

Purpose: Gets everyone in the group involved and keeps them active; offers practice in listening, learning names, focusing, communication and organization

Group Size: 10 to 30

Time: 10 – 15 minutes

Supplies: A variety of balls or other objects to toss (tennis balls, bean bags, squeaky toys, rubber chickens, Frisbees®, rubber balls, etc.)

Directions:

1. Group members stand in a circle.
2. Tell the group, "We are going to toss the ball in a set pattern, so that each person receives the ball once. I'm always going to toss the ball to [Name], who will then toss it to [Name], who tosses it to [Name]." Continue setting the pattern until everyone's name has been called and they've been tossed the ball. The last person should toss it back to you, the leader.
3. Practice tossing one of the objects through one cycle of the pattern to make sure it is set in everyone's mind.
4. Instruct the group to say aloud the name of the person to whom they are tossing the object. This helps get the other person's attention and also helps people remember the names of others in the group.
5. Start by throwing one of the objects, and then begin adding the other objects.
6. Continue until all the objects get back to you.
7. Process the activity in a way that enforces your desired outcome. Here are some sample questions:
   - What can we learn from this activity?
   - How can you relate this to organization (communication, listening skills)?
   - Why is it important to use someone's name?

Hands Down

Purpose: Gets a group to work together and solve a problem

Group Size: 4

Time: 10 minutes

Supplies: None

Directions:

1. Arrange students into groups of four (see *Getting into Groups* on pages 23-24 for suggestions).
2. Instruct groups that they must devise a way to support themselves one inch off the floor for five seconds with only hands touching the ground. Group members must be touching one another "so that a current of electricity could pass through your group." Objects such as chairs, walls and desks may not be used.

Solutions

Many creative solutions can be found. Two of the most common are:
- The group forms a square with each person face down and in a push-up position. Each person's feet are on another person's back. On the count of three, everyone "lifts," creating one big square push-up.
- The group forms a square, having each person sitting facing the side of another person in the square. Each person's legs are straight out with the feet resting on the next person's thighs. Everyone puts their hands behind them, and on the count of three, the whole group lifts up at once. Leverage is the key to this activity.

Home Sweet Home

Purpose: A self-awareness activity that provides a visual way to record and share important information about oneself

Group Size: 10 to 25

Time: 20 – 30 minutes

Supplies: Sheet of paper and a pencil for each student

Directions:

1. Have each person draw a large outline of a house. Include a door, at least two windows, a chimney, a sun and a cloud in the sky.
2. Ask students to think about some people and events that have influenced their lives. Give them some time to reflect before giving the following directions:

    - On the door, write the name of the person who always makes you feel at home.
    - On the bottom of the house, the foundation, write the name of the person who supports you the most.
    - On the roof, write the name of the person who helps you reach your dreams.
    - On the chimney, write something you want to tell the world.
    - On the sun, write what makes your days bright.
    - On the cloud, write one or more of your dreams.

3. When everyone is done, go around the circle and have each person share one of the items they wrote down and why. Do more if time permits.
4. If possible, hang the drawings in your classroom, and let others have a chance to read them.

Hot Beach Ball

Purpose: Provides a hands-on activity that combines movement with questions; helps everyone learn bits and pieces about each other

Group Size: 10 to 30

Time: 15 minutes

Supplies: Beach ball or other large ball

Directions:

1. The group stands in a circle with a little distance between each member.
2. Begin by asking a question and tossing the ball to another person. That person must answer the question and toss the ball to a new person, who answers the question and tosses the ball to another person. The ball gets tossed until everyone has answered the question. No one answers the same question twice.
3. The object is to keep the ball moving so no one is holding it more than three seconds. The questions have to be simple and not too in-depth.
4. To help keep things moving, have the students hold their hands up if they haven't had the ball yet and put them at their side once they've received that ball and answered the question.
5. Here are some sample questions:

    - What is your favorite color?
    - What was the last book you read?
    - Who is your favorite cartoon character?
    - What is a word beginning with G?
    - What is your favorite fruit?
    - What was the last song you heard?

How Many in Your Party?

Purpose: A good mixer that helps students learn more about their fellow group members
Group Size: 10 to 50
Time: 15 – 30 minutes
Supplies: None

Directions:

1. Explain that you are the maître d' at a fine restaurant and will be calling out seating arrangements for the group. Let the group mingle around the room a bit before you call out "Table for two (or three, or whatever number you choose)."
2. If you call out "table for two," group members pair off and introduce themselves. You will then give them a question to discuss at their "table." The first question could be "What are your favorite foods to eat?"
3. Give the groups a minute to discuss the question and then call out the next seating arrangement.
4. Each time, after the groups have formed, have them introduce themselves and discuss the question you give them.
5. Possible questions are:

    - What is something you really want to do in the next year?
    - What do you hope to get out of this class (workshop, meeting)?
    - Who can you always go to for good advice or a listening ear? Why?
    - What is your favorite thing to do outdoors?
    - What is your favorite season or holiday and why?
    - What talent would you really like to have?
    - What is/was your favorite Halloween costume?
    - When you have time to just sit and think, what do you think about?
    - Who should you write a letter or email to and why?
    - What is your favorite ride at an amusement park?

How Many Squares?

Purpose: Shows how working together can help achieve greater success and more accuracy; shows the difficulty of perceiving adequately
Group Size: Unlimited
Time: 10 minutes
Supplies: One copy of the How Many Squares? Worksheet and a pen or pencil per student

Directions:

1. Have each person count the squares on the worksheet (page 30) and write the answer on the page.
2. Break up the groups into threes, and have each group reach a consensus on how many squares they can find. (You should find 40 squares.)
3. Process the activity with the group:

    - How many squares did you count on your own?
    - How many squares did you count with your group?
    - Which count was more accurate? Why?
    - What advantages/disadvantages are there to working in a group?
    - In which way do you work best – in a group or alone? Why is that a good thing to know about yourself and to know about other people you may have to work with?

How Many Squares? Worksheet

Human Bridge

Purpose: To promote teamwork, trust and creative thinking
Group Size: 8 to 10
Time: 10 minutes
Supplies: Two chairs per group

Directions:

1. Groups of eight to ten people must form a bridge from one chair to the other "so the lightweight troll from another village can walk over them to the other side of the cliff and get the food needed to survive in the wilderness." However...

    - Only **4 hands** can be touching the ground.
    - Only **3 feet** can be touching the ground.
    - Only **2 rears** can be touching the ground.
    - Only **2 people** can be touching the chairs.

2. Let the group work for five minutes. If the challenge is too easy, take away a foot and/or a hand. If it is absolutely too hard, give them another five minutes and let them have another foot. The leader should use judgment to make the challenge fit the group.

3. After the bridge is completed, ask the students to process the activity:

    - Share stories about the activity.
    - Who took the role as the leader, and who were the followers?
    - Did anyone feel like their ideas were left out?
    - In what ways is being a team important?
    - How can building a human bridge relate to real life?

Human Treasure Hunt

Purpose: Forms and reforms many different groups of people in a short amount of time, providing an opportunity to get acquainted as quickly as possible
Group Size: 25 or more
Time: 5 – 10 minutes
Supplies: None

Directions:

1. All students should be in one large room or area.
2. You will be calling out various ways to organize into groups, and the students are to follow your directions each time. The idea is to get in as many groups as possible in a short amount of time.
3. If it is a very large group, use a microphone (if possible). Otherwise, blow a whistle each time a new formation is called out so that people will listen to the new direction.
4. Here are some ideas, but feel free to make up more as you go along:

   - Find someone with the same size thumb as you.
   - Find two other people who you don't know at all.
   - Find one other person with the same birth month as you.
   - Find three people whose favorite subject is different from yours.
   - Find two people who live 20 or more miles from you.
   - Find one person who likes the same sport as you.
   - Find four people who are wearing at least one item of clothing that is the same color as yours.
   - Find two people who have different brands or types of shoes than you.
   - Find a group of five who can and will sing "Row, Row, Row Your Boat" with you.
   - Find two other people and make the letter "W" with your arms.
   - Think of a number between one and ten. Find all the other people thinking of that number.

I Can Find That!

Purpose: Promotes teamwork; provides challenges that are harder than they appear to be
Group Size: 6 or more, depending on the size of the room
Time: 10 – 20 minutes
Supplies: Objects to hide around the room; an item sheet for each student

Directions:

1. Hide small objects around the room before anyone arrives. Be creative about hiding things, but make sure they remain in plain view so that nothing has to be disturbed.
2. Divide the large groups into smaller groups of two to four (see *Getting into Groups* on pages 23-24 for suggestions).
3. Give each student an item sheet (page 33) and tell them to find as many items on the list as possible before the time expires. Group members must stay together while searching for the objects.
   All objects found must be recorded on the sheet in order to get credit. No items are to be moved once they are spotted. Warn the students that they should try not to let on to other teams when or where they spot an item.
4. The team who finds the most items within the allotted time wins.
5. You can set the amount of time, but ten minutes is a good starting point.

I Can Find That! Worksheet

This is a game of searching, noticing, and finding. Here is a list of items you and your group members need to find and check off the list. Please write down where the item was found. All items are in this room. All are in plain view. You do not have to move anything to find these items. When you find an item, leave it where it is, and play it cool. Good luck!

Item: **Where Found:**

1. large paper clip _____
2. match _____
3. ruler _____
4. paper airplane _____
5. sunglasses _____
6. eraser _____
7. shiny confetti _____
8. penny _____
9. kazoo _____
10. balloon _____
11. lipstick container _____
12. runner band _____
13. band-aid _____
14. aspirin _____
15. button _____
16. spool of thread _____
17. key _____
18. postage stamp _____
19. thumbtack _____
20. nail _____

"I Didn't Know That"

Purpose: Similar to *People Bingo* on page 44, but requires some preliminary information and preparation

Group Size: 10 to 30

Time: 10 – 15 minutes

Supplies: "I Didn't Know That" Worksheet that you will create beforehand and a pen or pencil for each student

Directions:

1. Before this activity is used, you need to find out one funny or interesting fact about each person in the group. Make a grid worksheet incorporating these facts (see sample below), and make a copy for each person in the group.
2. At the beginning of the class, distribute the worksheets.
3. Tell the group members to mingle and ask one another questions to find out which fact fits which group member. When they have matched the correct person with the fact, have the person sign his or her name in the corresponding space.
4. Depending on your time and goal, you can end the activity after everyone gets a fully-signed worksheet, or you can encourage discussion of the various interests.

Sample "I Didn't Know That" Worksheet

collects comic books	has lived in Las Vegas	would love to have 50 cats
likes to paint	loves to watch cartoons	would love to be an actor
has 8 brothers and sisters	has never been to Disney World	belongs to the Medical Explorers Club
has milked cows by hand	owns a tarantula	has own webpage

I Gotta Hand It to You

Purpose: Provides a way to end a group session while focusing on something positive about each person
Group Size: 5 to 50
Time: 15 – 30 minutes
Supplies: Paper plate or sheet of paper and a marker (non-permanent) for each person; masking tape

Directions:

1. Give each student a paper plate or piece of paper.
2. Direct each student to trace one hand and to write his or her name on the plate.
3. Have students make loops of masking tape, and help one another tape the plates to their backs.
4. Then have everyone circulate and write on each other's plate something they like about or something positive they noticed about that person. Each student should sign his or her name to the note.
5. When the group is done, everyone will have an uplifting keepsake to take home with them.

Icebergs Ahead

Purpose: A good lesson in creative problem solving
Group Size: 15 to 25
Time: 15 – 30 minutes
Supplies: Tarp or blanket

Directions:

1. Lay the blanket on the ground. Explain that the group must get everyone aboard the ship (blanket/tarp) because the water is icy cold and they must survive the ocean voyage.
2. Set a time limit for getting everyone on the boat. The blanket should be a size that would allow the whole group to fit without too great of a challenge. Students are allowed to get on top of one another if you choose to allow it.
3. Tell the group they must all stay aboard for ten seconds (or about the time it takes to sing "Row, Row, Row Your Boat").
4. Next, inform the group that their boat just hit an iceberg and were all thrown off the boat. (They must get off the blanket now.)
5. Fold the blanket a little smaller and tell the group to re-board what's left of the boat. It should be a bit more difficult this time. They must stay on the boat for another ten seconds.
6. Again, the boat hits an iceberg. Everyone must get off the boat. Fold the blanket a little smaller and have the group try one more time to get everyone aboard the remaining planks for ten seconds. Make this last time very difficult by folding the blanket quite small.

Tip: It helps to have a couple of spotters, especially for the last round.

7. Process the activity:

    - What was the initial goal? How did it change?
    - What made the activity easy/difficult to do?
    - What actions do you take when you're dealing with setbacks?
    - Do you adjust easily to change? Why?
    - What feelings did you have during this activity? Can you relate those feelings to events that happen in everyday life?

Index Card Thing

Purpose: Provides students an opportunity to learn more about their fellow group members

Group Size: Unlimited

Time: 20 – 30 minutes

Supplies: An index card or sheet of paper and a pen or pencil for each student

Directions:

1. Have students write their answers to these six questions on the paper:

    a. What was your favorite childhood toy?
    b. What quality do you look for in a friend?
    c. What is the biggest problem in our society (school)?
    d. If you could have dinner with *anyone* in the world, who would it be?
    e. What advice would you give your parents (principal)?
    f. What three things would you like people to say about you?

2. After the questions are answered, everyone should pair off with a partner, introduce themselves and discuss their answers to questions A and B.
3. Next, one pair should team up with another pair, introduce themselves and discuss questions C and D.
4. Finally, one foursome teams up with another foursome, introduces themselves and discusses questions E and F.
5. Gauge the amount of time needed for the discussion of each set of questions.

"It Gives Me Great Pleasure to Introduce..."

Purpose: To get to know at least one person fairly well and then introduce that person to the rest of the group

Group Size: 6 to 20 (or unlimited if you want to skip the large-group introductions)

Time: 10 – 12 minutes

Supplies: An "It Gives Me Great Pleasure to Introduce..." Worksheet and a pen or pencil for each student

Directions:

1. Divide the group into pairs (See *Getting into Groups* on pages 23-24 for suggestions.) If you have an uneven number in the large group, have one group of three people.
2. Distribute the worksheets (page 37). Allow ten minutes for the students to fill in the information about their partners.
3. If time allows, have students introduce their partners to the rest of the group. If there is not time for this, then at least two people got to know each other better.

"It Gives Me Great Pleasure to Introduce..." Worksheet

"Our special guest today is [name] _____.

As you all know, [he or she] is widely known and highly acclaimed for [special accomplishments]
_____.

[Name] _____ has spent a great deal of time learning to _____

and recently demonstrated [his or her] powers of persuasion by convincing _____

to _____.

Our guest says [he or she] stays active by _____

and _____.

You may have read that [name] _____ recently added _____

and_____ to [his or her] material possessions and is planning to add

_____ in the near future.

One of the most enjoyable pastimes for [name] _____ is _____.

You can surely see that [name]_____ is a remarkable person.

It gives me great pleasure to introduce [name]_____."

JOY / GIVE

Purpose: Listen-and-learn activity during which group members share things about themselves; best done with people who know each other relatively well
Group Size: 6 to 25
Time: 20 – 30 minutes
Supplies: None

Directions:

1. Arrange the group in a circle.
2. Explain that this activity is called JOY, and it will provide a chance to share some events with the others in the group.
3. The letter J stands for *Just Did*. The first exercise then is to go around the circle and have each person share something that he or she *Just Did*. (There's no time frame set for *Just Did*. Students can interpret that however they like.)
4. The next letter is O, and it stands for *Ought To*. Starting with a different person, have each member tell about something he or she *Ought To* do.
5. The final letter is Y, which stands for *Yourself*. Again, starting with someone new, have each person tell the group something about him or herself.

Variation: GIVE
In place of the JOY, the letters in GIVE can be used as follows:

G   a *Goal* I recently accomplished
I   something in which I am very *Interested*
V   a strong *Value* in me (or something/someone I really *Value*)
E   something that really affects my *Emotions*

Just Like Clockwork

Purpose: Demonstrates how cooperation is necessary to achieve a common goal
Group Size: 20 to 100
Time: 15 minutes
Supplies: A stopwatch or clock to keep time

Directions:

1. Have everyone hold hands in a large circle.
2. Choose a person to be the starting point, and either put a marker there or stand there yourself.
3. Tell the group to move clockwise 360 degrees. When the starting person reaches the marker, the whole group should change direction and go 360 degrees counterclockwise. They are basically running in a circle one way and then back the other way.
4. Time the group to see how long it took them to complete the activity (one movement clockwise and one movement counterclockwise).
5. Then have them try it again to see if they can beat their previous record.
6. Continue trying to beat each previous record for as long as your time allows.

Knots

Purpose: Gets a group feeling relaxed and close
Group Size: 6 to 10
Time: 15 minutes
Supplies: None

Directions:

1. Have all group members stand in a circle. Students raise their hands in the air and grab the hands of other people in the group, keeping these restrictions in mind:

    - Each hand must connect to a different person.
    - No one can hold hands with the person on either side of them.

2. After everyone is connected, tell them to untangle without letting go of any hands.
3. The prize is the satisfaction of working together and solving the problem.

Line Up

Purpose: Shows that we can communicate in nonverbal ways
Group Size: 15 to 50
Time: 10 minutes
Supplies: None

Directions:

1. Tell the group to line up by birthday month and day (not year), so that January is on one side of the room and December is on the other. They *cannot* talk to one another while doing this.
2. Don't give students too many other directions. They'll figure out quickly how to work together and get the line correct.
3. When the group seems to be finished, have each person say his or her birthday month and day. Continue down the line to see if everyone is in order.
4. Process the activity:

    - Was this difficult for the group? Why or why not?
    - How did you communicate when you were told you couldn't talk?
    - Did a leader emerge from the group? Was that helpful? Why?
    - What would make this easier to do?

Variations: Line up by last names, shoe size, height, etc.

Lucky Thirteens

Purpose: Stresses cooperation and teamwork with any age group; basic addition skills when used with younger children
Group Size: 10 to 50, divided into teams of 4 or 5
Time: 5 – 10 minutes
Supplies: None

Directions:

1. Divide the group into teams of four or five (see *Getting into Groups* on pages 23-24 for suggestions).
2. Have the members of each team face one another and hold one fist out in front of them.
3. On the count of three, each team member holds up from zero to five fingers. The object is to have the total fingers held up equal thirteen. No one may talk or plan how to do this before the game starts. It will easily take a few tries to get the lucky thirteen.
4. Change the lucky number for another round.

The Mall Game

Purpose: Helps group members learn one another's names in a fast, fun and effective way
Group Size: 10 to 30
Time: 20 – 30 minutes
Supplies: None

Directions:

1. Ask the group to sit in a circle.
2. Tell everyone to imagine that they are shopping in a gigantic mall – a mall that has EVERYTHING! Each person needs to buy one item that begins with the first letter of his or her first name. Once everyone has thought of his or her item, the game begins.
3. Start by saying your own first name and the item you bought. For instance, I might say, "Patty Popcorn Popper." A variation is to add an action associated with your item while stating your name and item. I could quickly move my hands up and down in a jumping motion to represent the popcorn popper.
4. In turn, each person says his or her name and item and repeats the previous person's information. So, the second person would say "Jim Jack-in-the-Box, Patty Popcorn Popper."
5. Continue clockwise around the circle with everyone saying his or her name and item and repeating all previous information.
6. Since the first few people in the circle have fewer names and items to remember, and the last few people in the circle don't have their names repeated very often, you may want to go around the circle again and have each person repeat all the names and items one last time.
7. Remember that it is always okay to help people out if they forget any part of the information. We don't want to embarrass anyone; we want to learn names.

Variation: If the group is large, you may want to require that only the previous seven names be repeated.

Monster Walk

Purpose: Promotes teamwork, cooperation and creativity
Group Size: Unlimited, divided into teams of 5 to 10
Time: 10 minutes
Supplies: None

Directions:

1. Divide the group into teams of five to ten people (see *Getting into Groups* on pages 23-24 for suggestions).
2. Explain that each group must join themselves together to form a single monster that walks with both hands and feet on the ground. The monster must have one more foot and one less hand than the number of people in the group. For instance, if there are five people in the group, there must be six feet and four hands on the ground.
3. Once the monster is created, it must move five feet in any direction and make a sound.
4. Allow five to ten minutes for the groups to decide how to create their monsters.
5. Have each group go to the front of the room and demonstrate their monster walk.

Moose, Couch Potato, Mosquito

Purpose: Provides a quick energizer
Group Size: Unlimited
Time: 5 minutes
Supplies: None

Directions:

1. Have everyone pair off and stand with their backs to each other.
2. Explain that each person must decide, silently, if he or she is going to be a moose, couch potato or mosquito.
3. On the count of three, the partners should both turn around quickly and make the appropriate faces and arm motions:

   Moose: Hold up both hands on either side of head (like antlers).
   Couch Potato: Fold hands together on one side of head (sleeping).
   Mosquito: Pull down the skin under your eyes with pointer and middle finger on one hand; use other pointer finger to make a stinger alongside your nose

4. The game continues until both partners match when they turn around.
5. For an extra challenge, try it in groups of three.

Musical Chair Questions

Purpose: Gets a lot of boundary-breaking questions answered one-on-one in a short amount of time
Group Size: 14 to 50
Time: 20 minutes
Supplies: None

Directions:

1. Arrange the group into two concentric circles (an inner and outer circle) facing each other. Everyone should have a partner.
2. Ask a *Boundary-Breaking Question* from pages 11-12, and give the pairs one minute to talk about it. After the minute is up, give a direction such as "inner circle move 2 chairs to your left." The inner circle moves, and the leader asks a new question. Pairs are given a minute to talk. The activity continues in this manner.

Variation: To practice listening skills, designate the inner circle as the listeners and the outer circle as the talkers. Give the talker one minute to answer the question while the listener practices good listening skills. Switch roles after one minute.

Name Tag

Purpose: Helps group members learn more about one another and reflect on areas of common ground
Group Size: Unlimited
Time: 15 minutes
Supplies: 8 ½" x 11" paper for each student; markers; loops of tape

Directions:

1. Have everyone in the group make an oversized nametag with the following information on it: first and last name, favorite color, favorite subject, favorite movie and dream vacation. Encourage group members to use the whole sheet of paper, and set it up horizontally with their first names most prominent (see sample below).
2. After everyone has taped their name tags to their shirts, have group members mingle around the room and read one another's tags. Students cannot speak to anyone unless they have something in common on their tags.
3. If there is something in common, group members can talk about anything on the nametag. If nothing is in common, they can only read the tag and absorb the information without comment.
4. Process the activity with questions like:

   - What did you find out about others?
   - How did it feel when you found something in common with someone else?
   - How did it feel when you couldn't talk with certain people?

Example Name Tag:

Favorite Color		Favorite Subject
	First Name	
	Last Name	
Dream Vacation		Favorite Movie

Name This Tune

Purpose: Gets everyone involved through a challenging activity that uses a favorite medium – music

Group Size: Unlimited

Time: 15 minutes

Supplies: Music collection with 20 to 35 song snippets that you've pre-recorded (see note); one sheet of paper and pen or pencil for each group; device for playing the music

Directions:

1. Divide a large group in groups of four to six people (see *Getting into Groups* on pages 23-24 for suggestions).
2. Tell students that you are going to play a collection of song clips, and they are to write down the title and artist of each clip. You will play the songs from beginning to end one time only. The collection of songs will not be played a second time.
3. Give one point for each correct song title and one point for each correct artist.
4. When the music is done, read the correct answers. The group with the highest score wins.

Note: It is best to include all types of music – classical, rock, country, Christmas, jazz, blues, rap, – and from different eras. A fifteen second snippet is long enough. The library is a good resource for music that you may not have at home. The internet is a good source, too. Make a list of the song titles and artists in the order you recorded them. That will be your answer key. Don't allow a large gap of silence between songs – keep it moving along.

Newspaper Fashion Show

Purpose: Use organizational skills to accomplish a specific task

Group Size: 30 to 50, divided into groups of 6 to 10

Time: 30 – 40 minutes

Supplies: A stack of newspapers per group (about the size of an average metropolitan Sunday edition); masking tape

Directions:

1. Divide the larger group into smaller groups of six to ten people (see *Getting into Groups* on pages 23-24 for suggestions).
2. Tell each group to organize a fashion show, which the group creates using only newspaper, tape and their creativity.
3. Explain that each group must develop a theme for their show. (Examples: World of Weddings, Cartoon Capers, Costumes from Outer Space, The 1500s)
4. The groups must decide who will be the fashion designers and who will be the models.
5. Groups also need to decide who will emcee their show and who will write the exciting and detailed commentary.
6. Allow about 20 minutes for the planning and designing stage. At the end of this time, assemble everyone together and have each group present their show.
7. Time should be left at the end for processing the activity.

    - How did you come up with your ideas?
    - What organizational skills were used?
    - How was it decided which group member would do each task? Are some people better suited to certain tasks? Why? What does this tell you about organizing a group for a task?
    - What one thing did you learn from this activity?

People Bingo

Purpose: Helps group members mix and ask questions of one another
Group Size: 12 or more
Time: 10 minutes
Supplies: People Bingo Worksheet and pen or pencil for each student

Directions:

1. Give each student a worksheet (page 45) and a pen or pencil.
2. Instruct everyone to find a person that fits each description on the worksheet and have that person sign the appropriate square.
3. A person can sign another's paper only one time.
4. Allow enough time for everyone to fill their sheets.
5. At the end, ask the group "Whose name did you put down for 'Can Juggle'?" The group will shout out a few names. Have them come to the front and demonstrate with wads of paper or juggling balls. The same can be done for telling a joke, singing "Row, Row, Row Your Boat" and demonstrating CPR. (Avoid any demonstration of something that might result in injury, such as doing cartwheels.)

Personal Crest

Purpose: Gives everyone a chance to visually and verbally explain who they are and what they stand for
Group Size: 5 to 25
Time: 20 minutes, plus time for discussion
Supplies: A Personal Crest Worksheet and a pen or pencil for each student

Directions:

1. Give everyone a worksheet (page 46). Explain that the crest will become a symbol for the things that are important to each of them.
2. The crest is divided into seven sections, with each one representing something different. Information can be recorded by either drawing or writing.
3. Give the following directions:

    a. In section I, write three things you really like about yourself.
    b. In section II, list the people who have influenced your life.
    c. In section III, tell about an event that has been a turning point in your life.
    d. In section IV, write down three things for which you are thankful.
    e. In section V, write a favorite quote that guides your life.
    f. In section VI, tell about what you believe in and stand for.
    g. In section VII, explain your passion and purpose in life as you see it now.

4. Ask the students to share portions of their crest entries with the group. Allow students to ask questions of one another. This may help further clarify to the students who they are and what they stand for.
5. The crests can be hung in the room for everyone to see or can be explained and taken home as a reminder for each person to stand up for what he or she believes.

People Bingo Worksheet

can juggle	saw a live concert in the past year	plays a fall sport	wears the same size shoe as you do
will sing "Row, Row, Row Your Boat" for you	has been to the movies in the last 2 weeks	read 3 or more books in the past 3 months	hates to mow the lawn
has been in a drama production	can cook a basic meal	has held a part-time job	favorite food is pizza
has a birthday in the same month as you	can tell you what CPR stands for	went to 3 or more baseball games this year	can do a cartwheel
knows a clean joke	has brown eyes	reads the comics in the newspaper	watches a reality show

Personal Crest Worksheet

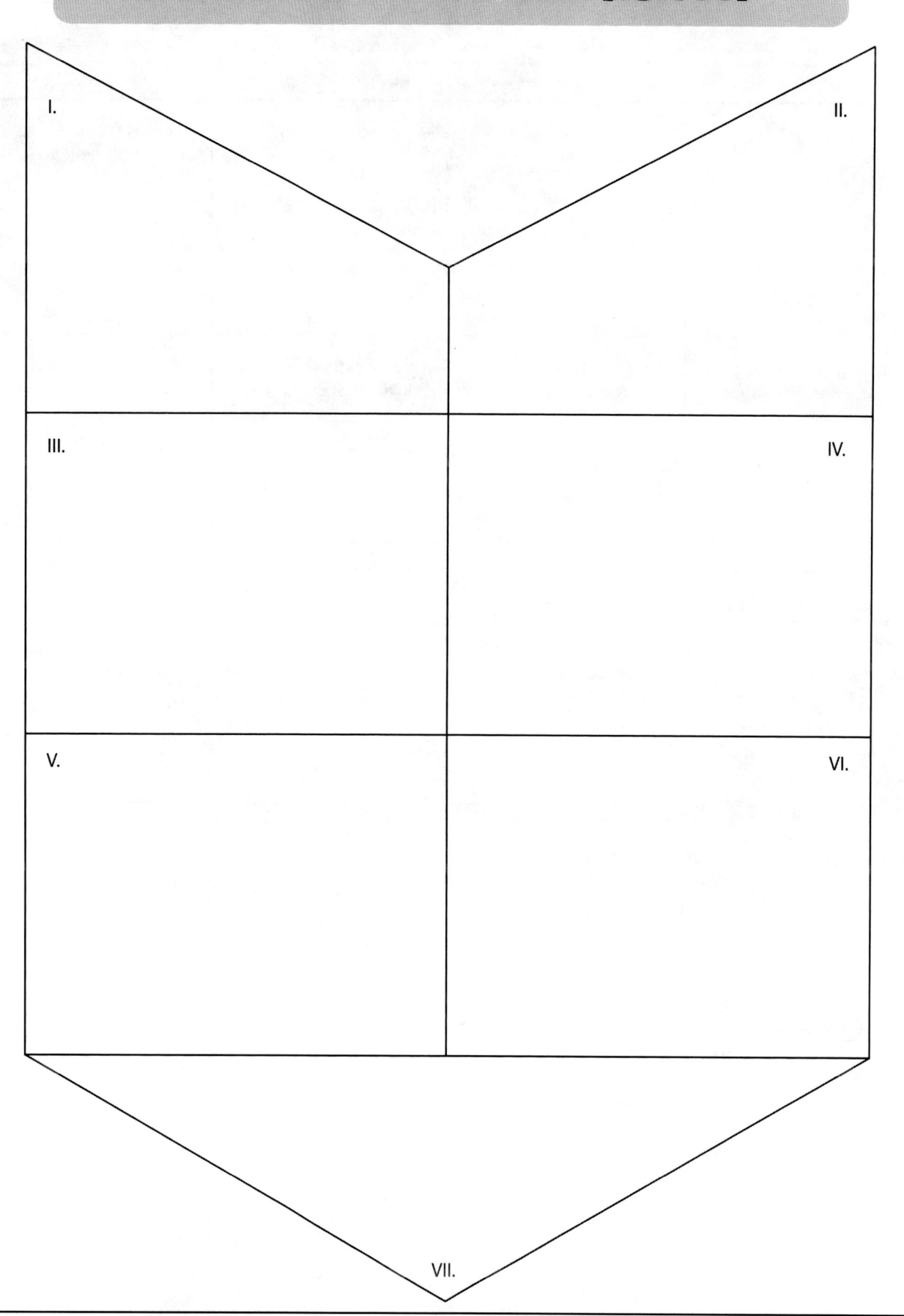

I.

II.

III.

IV.

V.

VI.

VII.

Picture Proverbs

Purpose: Uses visual clues for a guessing game about well-known proverbs; can be done as a competition between two teams or as a whole-group activity

Group Size: 10 to 25

Time: 15 minutes

Supplies: Proverbs cut apart into slips and folded; paper and markers or chalkboard and chalk; stopwatch; hat or other container

Directions:

1. Put the folded proverb slips into a hat or another container.
2. Divide the group into two teams.
3. Team A selects someone to draw the first proverb. He or she picks a proverb out of the hat and begins drawing. No written words from the proverb may appear in the drawing, only pictures representing the words.
4. Time how long it takes Team A to guess the proverb. Record the number of seconds.
5. Team B selects a representative to pick a proverb and draw it. Record the time it takes Team B to guess the answer.
6. The turn goes back to Team A, which selects a second person to draw. Continue alternating teams until all proverbs are used.
7. The team with the lowest total time is the winner.

Variation: Do the activity without the competition. Select the appropriate number of group members to draw the proverbs and let everyone guess together. Demonstrate that you don't have to be an artist to get your ideas across.

Don't cry over spilt milk.

He who laughs last, laughs best.

A bird in the hand is worth two in the bush.

A stitch in time saves nine.

Don't put the cart before the horse.

Money is the root of all evil.

Too many cooks spoil the broth.

Look before you leap.

The early bird catches the worm.

Steady wins the race.

People who live in glass houses shouldn't throw stones.

Hear no evil, see no evil, speak no evil.

You will be judged by the company you keep.

Do as I say, not as I do.

Think before you speak.

Absence makes the heart grow fonder.

Out of sight, out of mind.

Every cloud has a silver lining.

Laugh, and the world laughs with you; cry, and you cry alone.

Beauty is in the eye of the beholder.

To err is human, to forgive, divine.

Monkey see, monkey do.

Pipe Dreams

Purpose: An exercise for setting realistic goals and reaching them
Group Size: 5 to 50
Time: 15 minutes
Supplies: A pipe cleaner (or chenille stem) for each person in the group

Directions:

1. Discuss the idea of setting personal goals. Goals are dreams with deadlines. If we write down our goals we'll have a better chance of achieving them.
2. Goals don't work unless they are "SMART" goals, an acronym for these characteristics:

   Specific
   Measurable
   Attainable
   Responsible
   Timely

3. Give examples:

   - If I want to be an Olympic gymnast and I'm forty years old, that is not a very SMART goal.
   - If I want to attend the gymnastic finals at the next Olympics, that is a SMART goal because it is realistic and attainable if I do some planning.

4. Give each member a pipe cleaner.
5. Tell them to decide on a goal that they would like to accomplish this school year (or by next week, before this class is over, etc.).
6. Make sure students apply the SMART philosophy to their goals. Have them write it out if you'd like.
7. Have group members form symbols out of the pipe cleaners that will remind them of their goals.
8. Each person should share his or her goal with the group. The group can challenge the SMART aspects of the goal to help each member clarify what they hope to achieve.

Positive Name Exchange

Purpose: Offers an exercise for looking at the good in others and feeling good about yourself
Group Size: 5 to 20
Time: 10 minutes
Supplies: Paper and pencil for each student

Directions:

1. Distribute a piece of paper and pencil to each person in the group.
2. Each person should write his or her first name vertically down the left side of the paper.
3. Everyone passes their papers to the left. Each group member writes something positive about the person whose paper they have that begins with one of the letters of his or her name.
4. Pass the papers again. Now the next person writes something positive using one of the remaining letters in the person's name.
5. Keep passing the sheets of paper until all letters in everyone's name are filled up with uplifting comments.
6. Return the sheets to their owners, who should keep them as a reminder of the good things that happened in the group. Or, you can have the last person to write on the sheet read that person's compliments to the rest of the group.

Example for the name BRENDA:

Believes in other people
Remembers my birthday
Enjoys helping others
Never brags about her music ability
Doesn't make fun of others
Always has a smile on her face

Promise Rings

Purpose: Good activity for when a group disbands (either temporarily, like at the end of a retreat, or permanently, like at graduation)
Group Size: Unlimited, but this is best done with a group of people who know each other well
Time: 20 – 30 minutes, depending on group size
Supplies: An inexpensive gold or silver ring (they can be found at party supply stores everywhere) for each person

Directions:

1. Give everyone a ring, but tell them not to put it on yet.
2. Explain that these are promise rings, and that each person is to think of something they want to promise to do or to follow through on after the group disbands (graduates, goes home, breaks camp, ends retreat, etc.). Point out that while belonging to a group, each person learns something about the others and about himself or herself. Many times, through the course of being a member of a group, a person sets a goal or gets an idea for something. It could be to meet a new person or write a letter to someone. It could be to help out at a soup kitchen or to be more patient with their siblings.
3. After everyone has thought for a few minutes, ask them to share their promises with the group. As each person shares the promise, tell him or her to put on the ring.
4. Everyone should wear their rings home as a reminder of their promises.

Punch Ball Questions

Purpose: An interactive, get-to-know-you activity
Group Size: 10 to 25
Time: 15 minutes
Supplies: Punch ball with questions already written on it

Directions:

1. Arrange the group in a circle.
2. Tell everyone that you will start tossing the punch ball around. When the ball is caught, the group member must answer the question that is closest to his or her right thumb.
3. Make sure everyone gets the punch ball once before someone gets it a second time. To help keep track of this, when the ball is being tossed, those who have not had it yet should hold their hands up. Those who have already received the ball should keep their hands at their sides.
4. Use your own questions or the *Boundary-Breaking Questions* on pages 11-12. Pick the lighter-weight questions so the game moves along quickly.

Rapid Juggle
(a variation of *Group Juggle-Toss*)

Purpose: Promotes working together to streamline a task and think beyond the obvious to solve a problem
Group Size: 10 to 30
Time: 10 minutes
Supplies: One ball or object to toss

Directions:

1. Establish a pattern of tossing as described in the *Group Juggle-Toss* game (see page 27). Go through one cycle of tossing in that pattern.
2. Now tell students that you are going to time them to see how fast they can finish the tossing pattern.
3. After you establish the time for that first round, ask if they can think of anything they can do to speed up the toss.
4. Try one of the ideas and time it.
5. Again, challenge them to come up with a way to do it even faster. Continue this until you've done it about as fast as you think is possible. The fastest way I've seen it done is when they figure out that they can rearrange themselves to be next to the person they would toss to. Then they end up just passing the object from one to another around the circle. I don't give them any hints for this arrangement, though, and they feel pretty good when they come up with it on their own.
6. Process the activity:

    - What can we learn from this activity?
    - How can we relate this to "real life" (our role as peer helper, leader, advisor, club member, family member)?
    - How did you feel after each attempt at cutting down the time?

Rock, Paper, Scissors Train

Purpose: Provides an opportunity for everyone to get involved and be a winner
Group Size: 50 or more
Time: 5 – 10 minutes
Supplies: None

Directions:

1. Make sure everyone understands the basics of the game *Rock, Paper, Scissors*. A closed fist indicates "rock." A flat hand indicates "paper." Holding up the index and middle finger on one hand indicates "scissors." Two players each make three chopping motions with one of their arms, and at the end of the third chop, they reveal which of the three options they chose by showing a fist, a flat hand, or two fingers. The winner is assessed as follows: Rock crushes scissors. Scissors cuts paper. Paper covers rock.
2. Have everyone find a partner.
3. Explain that when you say, "Go," each pair does a *Rock, Paper, Scissors* game. Whoever loses puts his or her hands on the shoulders of the winner and starts a "train."
4. That train of two players then pairs with another two-person train.
5. Now the train leaders play *Rock, Paper, Scissors*. The losing train joins the winning train and forms a four-person train. The four-person train pairs with another four-person train. This pattern continues until there are just two long trains left.
6. Make a big deal about the final round between the last two trains. The excitement of the team that wins is overwhelming. Even though nearly everyone has already lost the game, they end up rooting for their new team. We all love to be part of the winning team.
7. Have the team that loses the last round join the winning team and let the train do a victory lap. Play "The Locomotion" or some other fun music and enjoy.
8. Most groups want to do this activity repeatedly.

Rope Writing

Purpose: Emphasizes team cooperation
Group Size: 8 to 20
Time: 15 minutes
Supplies: 40 to 50 feet of rope or twine; blindfolds (or have everyone close their eyes)

Directions:

1. After making sure that everyone is blindfolded, hand each person a section of the rope, making sure everyone is equidistant from one another.
2. Explain that the group is to form a shape, letter, or short word that you call out. Players are not to drop their sections of the rope. When the group thinks they are done, one person in the group can let go of the rope and, still blindfolded, can feel his or her way around it. This group member can instruct the rest of the players how to adjust themselves in order to make the shape more accurate.
3. When the first shape is complete, have the group assess how they did and what would improve their performance. Then call out a new shape and see how the group works together this time.
4. Discuss the idea of cooperation and teamwork. Include the points: sometimes you have to trust that the other group members are doing their job, even if you don't see them doing the work; and everyone in a group must do their best, even if no one is watching.

Variation: Do the activity in the same way, but this time, instead of the blindfolds, tell the group that they cannot talk to each other. They have to use nonverbal communication. Ask them how not being able to talk helps or hinders their task. Discuss other ways that we communicate.

Rumors

Purpose: Demonstrates how communication can get distorted and rumors start and spread

Group Size: 10 to 30

Time: 15 minutes

Supplies: A copy of the Rumors Worksheet and a pen or pencil for each student

Directions:

1. Have five people leave the room. Tell them they will come back one by one to hear a story later; this is all they need to know.
2. Select two students to play the roles of Ben and Sue. Give them each a copy of the script, and have them read their parts out loud. Tell the rest of the group to listen carefully to the story.
3. When the story is finished, have one of the five people who are outside of the room come back. Tell the person who just returned to listen carefully to the details of the story that will be told.
4. Select one person who listened to the story to tell it to the person who just returned to the room. The storyteller should include as much detail as possible.
5. Give the rest of the people in the room a copy of the story, and tell them to read the story silently as the storyteller is speaking. Ask students to pay careful attention to the parts being left out.
6. The person who was just told the story now becomes the storyteller, and he or she must pass on the story to the next person brought back into the room. This pattern continues until all five people have heard the story.
7. The last person to hear the story then relates it to the whole group.
8. Next, have Ben and Sue reread the original script.
9. Process the activity:

    - How did the story change as it was repeated?
    - What were some details that were left out?
    - Is this story typical of something you might overhear? Why?
    - Did anyone add details that were never in the original story? Do people you know ever do that? Why?
    - How can you relate this to gossip and rumors in your school, group of friends, or work place?
    - If you hear rumors, what's the appropriate thing to do? How do you avoid getting into a situation like this?
    - Why is it hard to remember all of the details?
    - Has any rumor been told about you? How did that make you feel?

Note: Remind the group that the distortions that developed during this activity were not the fault of the people who left the room. Everyone just needs to remember the human tendency to forget details and to be sure to learn the real story before repeating any details.

Rumors Worksheet - The Story

Sue: What did you do this weekend, Ben?

Ben: Well, it wasn't too exciting. On Saturday, a bunch of us hung out at the mall since it was raining. What'd you do?

Sue: Well, we were supposed to have a softball game at noon on Saturday, and even though it was raining lightly, we were all out there ready to play. Then it turns out that the other team thought the game was cancelled, so they never showed up. And I missed out on a camping trip with my cousin just to play in the stupid game.

Ben: It wasn't too exciting at the mall either. A bunch of us were going to go to a movie, but we couldn't decide what to see. Then Amy, Jennifer and Kate showed up, and they were trying to convince us to go see "Lost in the Ozone." We didn't really want to see that, but you know how Mike sorta likes Amy, so he tried to convince her to come with us. Well, then the other two got mad. It was really a pain.

Sue: Boy! Then I guess I'm glad I wasn't there. Our coach ended up taking us to Pizza Place for lunch, which was really fun, but while we were eating, someone backed their car into his van. Then I had to call my parents to come pick me up because our coach had to wait for the police to come.

Ben: Well, maybe next weekend we can find something fun to do!

Sandwich Cookie Solutions

Purpose: Stresses the importance of planning, organizing and working together
Group Size: 10 to 50, divided into groups of 5 or 6
Time: 20 – 45 minutes
Supplies: One pack of sandwich cookies for each group, or other building supplies (see suggestions below)

Directions:

1. Divide the large group into teams of five or six people (see *Getting into Groups* on pages 23-24 for suggestions). Keeping the teams small gives everyone a chance to be involved.
2. Decide the goal of this activity ahead of time. Some ideas include building the tallest structure, building the most creative structure, using the white filling in the most unusual way, or to create a machine that will solve one of the world's problems.
3. Give the groups about five minutes to plan before you distribute the supplies (otherwise players may get right to work before planning what they want to do).
4. Allow ten to twenty minutes for the groups to finish their creations.
5. Have each group present and explain their finished product to the large group.
6. You can judge who did the best job of reaching the goal, or let the groups vote.
7. Process the activity when you are done:

   - Did your creation turn out the same way as you planned it in the beginning?
   - How did you come up with your idea?
   - What were some, if any, difficulties you encountered?
   - How would you do this activity differently next time?
   - Were you happy with the outcome?
   - What is the advantage to planning the activity before you begin?
   - Did you all agree on what the outcome would be?
   - How can you relate this to things you do every day?

Other Building Supplies:
   - straws and tape
   - graham crackers and frosting
   - newspaper and tape
   - things found in the recycling bin (various paper and cardboard)
   - different types of pasta
   - marshmallows and toothpicks
   - a bag of supplies you give each team (10 paperclips, 10 index cards, 2 milk jugs, strips of construction paper, a yard of masking tape, 15 spaghetti noodles, etc.)

Send Me Your Champion

Purpose: Provides a team competition activity in which the whole group must get involved; lots of spirited competition

Group Size: at least 3 teams of 15 to 30 people each

Time: 15 minutes

Supplies: Qualifications list (See below for starters, and then add your own if you wish)

Directions:

1. Have each group huddle together, ready to create their champion.
2. Begin the game by saying, "Send me your champion who has [fill in the qualification]."
3. The first team to send up a person who fits all of the qualifications is the winner for that round. Play until a certain number of points are reached or until you don't want to play another round.
4. The team-building experience is what this activity is about. Discuss in the end how important it was to listen to all directions before "building" your champion. Sometimes we are so eager to begin that we don't wait to get the whole picture. Then we miss some vital information, and we can't successfully complete our tasks or projects.

Ideas for Qualifications:

- Send me your champion who has on four necklaces, a ring on each finger of the right hand, one sock on the left foot, and is hopping up and down on the right foot.
- Send me your champion who has on two hats, shirtsleeves rolled up, two left shoes, and is holding hands with someone else on the team.
- Send me your champion who is a male, wearing three watches on his left arm, a pair of jeans with both pant legs rolled up, and is reciting nursery rhymes.
- Send me your champion who is female, wearing three hats, a toe ring, no socks, but a shoe on one foot and a sandal on the other.

Simpler Qualifications:

- Send me your champion holding a shoelace that is not in a shoe.
- Send me two of your champions – one must have a text on a cell phone from the other saying "U R GR8."
- Send me your champion wearing two left shoes.
- Send me your champion who is holding a penny, a nickel, and a dime.
- Send me your champion who is holding someone else's driver's license.
- Send me your champion who has six socks on one foot.
- Send me your whole group lined up shortest to tallest, hands by your sides, and perfectly silent.

Sentence Structure

Purpose: Utilizes organizational skills, thinking-on-your-feet strategies, and cooperation; teamwork
Group Size: 15 to 30 (can be done with larger groups if you make more than two teams)
Time: 10 minutes
Supplies: Newsprint and washable markers for each team

Directions:

1. Tape a sheet of newsprint to the wall for each team, or lay the sheets on the floor. Allow room between the sheets of paper so each team will have its own space. Check to see that the markers won't run through the paper and get on the wall or floor.
2. Divide the group into equal teams, and have each team line up about 15 feet away from the paper.
3. Each team member must go to the paper, write a word that will help form a complete sentence, hand off the marker to the next team member, and go to the back of the line.
4. Each person gets to write only one word. The last person to write must complete the sentence. (If there are nine people on each team, the sentence should be nine words long.)
5. No group member may talk to any other member while the sentence is being formed.
6. The first team to write a complete sentence is the winner of that round.
7. It's a good idea to give the groups a topic for each sentence, especially if you're working with a younger group.
8. Process the activity:

   - What made this difficult/easy to do?
   - Did you like the outcome of your sentences? Why?
   - How did teamwork come into play in this activity?
   - In this activity you had to think quickly about what word you were going to add to the sentence. In what other areas of your life do you have to think on your feet?
   - Do you like having to think about/decide things quickly? Why or why not?

Variation: Have the team write a story in this same fashion. The winner can be the team with the most creative story, or the team that used the most words in their story in the given amount of time.

Shoes!

Purpose: Provides an active way to get everyone relaxed and less self-conscious
Group Size: 15 to 50
Time: 10 minutes
Supplies: None (but everyone must have on a pair of shoes)

Directions:

1. Arrange the group in either one big circle or a few small circles.
2. Have everyone take off their right shoe and toss it into the center of the circle.
3. When you say "Go," everyone should grab someone else's shoe and put it on.
4. Then have students line up by pairing up the shoes. Each person has to cross his or her right leg over someone else's left leg to make a pair.
5. End by having everyone introduce themselves to their "shoemates."

Shut Eye Drawings

Purpose: Prompts discussion about seeing the big picture and making assumptions about ourselves and our lives; produces some funny artwork

Group Size: Unlimited

Time: 10 minutes

Supplies: Paper and pencil for each person

Directions:

1. Tell everyone that they are going to draw a picture, and that you will tell them what to draw.
2. Instruct students to close their eyes and *keep them closed* while they are drawing.
3. Use the following list for things to draw. Make sure you read them in order, and allow enough time in between items for the students to draw each picture.

    a. the outline of a house
    b. a big tree next to the house
    c. two windows in the house
    d. a nest in the tree
    e. a door on the house
    f. sun in the sky
    g. chimney on the house
    h. two birds in the nest
    i. smoke coming out of the chimney

4. It adds to the fun if you ham it up when you mention each new item. Pretend that you don't realize that you're making everyone go back and forth to different parts of their pictures. There are lots of moans and groans when they have to find the right place to add the next item.
5. When you are finished with the list, tell everyone to open their eyes and look at their masterpieces.
6. Have everyone hold up their artwork for all to see.
7. Process the activity with the following analogy:

Sometimes it's hard to get our lives right if we can't see the big picture. Just like in our drawing, things can be out of place and less than perfect. But if we can open our eyes to the situations and happenings around us, we can see our way more clearly and can make the necessary adjustments before our lives get too fragmented or off track.

- What can make your life seem fragmented?
- What or who helps you see the bigger picture?
- What assumptions do we make about others' lives?
- How can we help one another get on the right track?

Skittergories

Purpose: A large group activity that gets people mixing with one another quickly
Group Size: 50 to 125
Time: 20 – 30 minutes
Supplies: An index card (or slip of paper) for each person

Directions:

1. Prepare by writing one item from a specific category on each card (see suggestions below). The number of items in a category should correspond to the number of students you want in each group. Seven to ten is usually a good choice.
2. Give all group members a card, and instruct them to keep the cards to themselves until each person has one.
3. When you say, "Go," students are to try to find all of the other people who fit into their same category. This group then becomes a team.
4. After everyone has found his or her group, read the category lists aloud to be sure someone is not on the wrong team.
5. Give each team seven minutes to prepare a short skit that relates their category and each item in their category to a theme of your choice – leadership, service, reaching out to others, communication skills, etc.
6. Have each team present their skit for the whole group.

Category Ideas

States
Colorado
Wisconsin
Alabama
Rhode Island
Montana
Texas
West Virginia
Oklahoma

Sports
baseball
basketball
football
soccer
volleyball
golf
gymnastics
track

Trees
pine
spruce
elm
maple
birch
oak
walnut
willow

Flowers
rose
zinnia
carnation
daisy
aster
marigold
tulip
lily

Colors
blue
aqua
red
orange
purple
yellow
brown
green

Holidays
Easter
Groundhog Day
St. Patrick's Day
Christmas
Thanksgiving
Valentine's Day
Hanukkah
Halloween

Other good categories include candy bars, cereal brands, cheeses, song titles, vehicles, and tourist attractions.

SOS

Purpose: Provides an outdoor exercise in overcoming adversity through teamwork
Group Size: 8 to 30
Time: 15 – 30 minutes
Supplies: Twigs, rocks, and branches; blindfolds

Directions:

1. Divide the group into teams of six to eight members (see *Getting into Groups* on pages 23-24 for suggestions).
2. Explain that each team is stranded on a desert island. Their goal is to build a large SOS sign on the ground so that low-flying planes will see it and rescue the group. The catch is that each team member is impaired in a specific way. One-third of the members of each team are blindfolded. One-third can't use their arms and must keep their hands in their pockets or at their sides. The last third of the team members cannot speak. Everyone must be included in the project for it to be a success.
3. Once the instructions are given, let each team get to work. If there is more than one group working on this at a time, make sure they are separated a bit so they don't see how other groups are solving the problem.
4. When the SOS sign is complete, process the activity:

    - How did you deal with each person's impairment and include him or her in the activity?
    - Was this easy or difficult to do? Why?
    - What did you learn from this activity that you can relate to other situations in your life?

Sound Off

Purpose: Invites people to step out of their comfort zones, but provides lots of fun; best played with a group who knows one another at least a little
Group Size: 10 to 20
Time: 5 – 10 minutes
Supplies: None

Directions:

1. Direct the group to sit in a circle.
2. Tell everyone that no one is to laugh during this activity. Anyone who laughs is out of the game. The last person to remain in the circle is the winner.
3. Going counter clockwise, have the person on your right start the game by passing a sound of some kind – a sniff, a snort, a hiccup, a squeal – to the person on his or her right. That person then passes the sound along to the next person, and it continues around the circle. If anyone laughs at any time, that person is out of the game.
4. When the sound gets back to you, the round is over.
5. Now have the person to your right make a new sound, and pass it to the person on his or her right. Continue until it gets back to the second leader. That round is over, and you can start a third round. Remember that if anyone laughs, he or she is out of the game.
6. Continue until all but one person is eliminated.

Note: The sound-maker may add facial expressions, and the group must copy those as well as the sound.

Spider Web

Purpose: Uses problem-solving skills; designed so that all members feel comfortable taking part

Group Size: 15 to 25

Time: 20 – 30 minutes

Supplies: Yarn or string to make the spider web; two trees about 10 feet apart (if done outside) or two poles (if done inside)

Directions:

1. The set up for this activity needs to be done ahead of time. Assemble the spider web by first tying the string from one tree to another at an eight-foot height, and then tying another string at ground level. This is the beginning of the web.

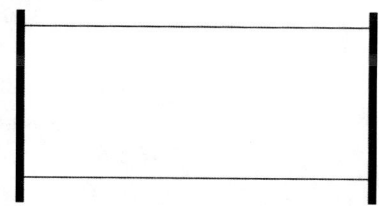

2. Next, tie off sections to make holes big enough for people to step through or be lifted through. Count the number of people who have to get through the web and keep that in mind when deciding how many holes to make. Remember to make a couple of holes a bit more difficult than others or the group won't be challenged enough. Don't provide too many easy options. The spider web should look something like the sketch below when you're finished.

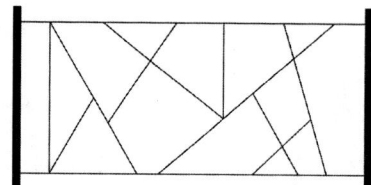

3. The rule is that each hole can only be used three times (four if you have a larger group). The students have to plan and keep track of how many times a hole is used.
4. The object of this activity is to get all players from one side of the spider web to the other by either crawling through on their own or being lifted through by others. Planning and trust are a part of this activity; without them it cannot be successfully completed.
5. Be sure to use a large gym mat under the spider web. Talk about safety before you start the activity. Someone always has to be a spotter when people are being lifted.
6. Set up the scenario with the group with a story similar to the following: A pack of angry gazelles is after your group, and you must run to safety. The only way to get to the safe area is to go through the poisonous spider web. The group must get everyone through before they can go on. No one can touch any part of his or her body or clothing to the web, or they will become motionless for one minute and cannot be passed through the web. Try to save everyone before the angry gazelles get to you.
7. Step back and watch the group plan and execute their ideas. Remind them that each hole can only be used three times.
8. You can set a time limit if you want to put a little pressure on the group; 15 to 30 minutes is usually enough time.
9. Process the activity:

   - How did you go about planning out this activity?
   - Did everyone get a chance to share their ideas? Is that good or bad?
   - Did anyone emerge as a leader?
   - Was it easy to trust the people lifting you through the web? Why?
   - Did you run into any problems?
   - Did everyone get over safely?
   - In what other real-life situations might you have to trust someone else to make a plan or help you through a situation?

Story Line

Purpose: Creates a memorable experience in working together; writing a story with a moral
Group Size: Unlimited, divided into teams of 3 or 4
Time: 30 minutes
Supplies: Paper and pencil for each group

Directions (Version 1):

1. Direct each group to write a story with a moral (lesson) using these 20 key words: sun, car, laughter, dark, social, two, walk, airplane, silly, blink, priceless, map, turn, pocket, run, book, pool, create, hand, fire. The words must be used in order. Other words may, of course, come in between these key words, but as the story unfolds, the word *sun* must come first, *car* next, *laughter* next, and so on.
2. Allow ten minutes for writing.
3. Have each group read its story when all are finished.
4. Process the activity:

   - Why was this easy/difficult?
   - How did you decide what to write about?
   - Were you surprised by the outcome of any of the stories? Why?
   - Which story did you like the best? Why?
   - Do you like working by yourself or with a group when doing activities like this? Why?
   - What are some characteristics you need to work successfully in a group?

Directions (Version 2):

1. Have each group list 20 TV show titles. Give the groups three minutes to make their lists. Don't tell them what they're going to do with the titles.
2. When the groups have finished, tell them they have to write a story with a moral using all of the titles they listed. The titles can be used in any order. Read the titles aloud to the group, and see if the members can mentally note all 20 of the TV titles.
3. Process the activity as in Version 1.

Story Time

Purpose: Establishes a fun atmosphere in which everyone contributes an idea
Group Size: 5 to 25
Time: 10 – 15 minutes
Supplies: Any item to toss safely (for example – a hat, stuffed animal or roll of tape)

Directions:

1. Arrange the group in a circle.
2. Ask for a volunteer to start the story.
3. The volunteer holds the object while saying the first line of a story. For example, "It was a dark and stormy night. I was sitting on the edge of my bed when a shadow in the shape of a ..."
4. Then the storyteller tosses the object to another person, who has to pick up the story right where it was stopped. The second person adds a few lines before passing the object to someone else.
5. The goal is to keep the story going no matter how quickly the object is being tossed around.

Strength Bombardment

Purpose: Gives individuals a chance to hear positive things that others have to say about them; to say positive things about others; should be done with students who know one another fairly well

Group Size: 5 to 20

Time: 30 – 90 minutes depending on the group size

Supplies: None

Directions:

1. Arrange the group in a circle, with one member sitting in the center. If group members feel uncomfortable sitting in the middle of the circle, they may remain on the outside of the circle.
2. Each member of the circle should say a few positive words about the group member in the center. Comments should be brief (10 to 20 seconds) and specific. (I often outlaw the words *neat, cool* and *nice*.)
3. The person in the middle may only respond with "Thank You." He or she may not dispute what has been said. (Sometimes it is hard to accept compliments.)
4. Continue until all members have had a chance to be "bombarded" with strengths.

Talking Buddies

Purpose: Provides practice in good listening and sharing skills; there are no incorrect answers, only honest and dishonest ones

Group Size: 2 or more

Time: 30 minutes

Supplies: Sheet with discussion questions

Directions:

1. Have everyone pair off. If there are an odd number of students, one group should have three people.
2. One person in each pair is designated the listener, and the other is the speaker. (I often help this process along by saying that the person with the longest hair, the tallest person, or the smallest shoe size is the speaker.)
3. The speaker is to choose one of the questions and spend three minutes sharing an answer. When the three minutes are up, players switch roles and the listener becomes the speaker. Allow another three minutes for this.
4. After the first question has been answered by each person in the pair, they should choose another question and begin again.
5. If space is available, have the pairs go off to a quieter place to discuss the questions.
6. Continue the activity until the allotted time is up.

Talking Buddies Questions
- If you could have lived in a different time in history, when would it have been and why?
- What is something that you have worked hard for, and you are proud of?
- If a crystal ball could tell you the truth about any one thing you wished to know about your future, what would you want to know?
- If you could wake up tomorrow having gained one ability or quality, what would it be?
- What would constitute a "perfect evening" for you?
- Your house, containing everything you own, catches fire. After saving your loved ones and pets, you have time to safely make a final dash to save any item. What would it be? What makes this item so significant?
- If you could interview any person who has ever lived, who would it be and why?
- What world event so far in your life has affected you the most? How?
- What would you like to be doing ten years from now?

Teamwork - LOGOS

Purpose: Offers a fun way to see the value of cooperation
Group Size: Unlimited, divided into groups of 4 or 5
Time: 10 minutes
Supplies: A logo sheet and a pen or pencil for each team

Directions:

1. Divide each large group into smaller groups of four or five (see *Getting into Groups* on pages 23-24 for suggestions).
2. Make a logo sheet by cutting out recognizable letterhead or logos from well-known companies or events. Paste them on a sheet of paper and leave space beneath each logo for writing. Make a copy of the sheet for each team.
3. When the group gathers, break students into teams and distribute the logo sheets. Allow five to ten minutes for them to identify as many logos as possible.
4. The group with the most correct answers in the winner.

Ten Nouns

Purpose: Helps define the concept of self-interest; helps individuals discover what motivators are at work within themselves and others in a group
Group Size: 6 to 25
Time: 20 – 40 minutes
Supplies: 8 ½" x 11" paper, a pen or pencil, and a marker for each person

Directions:

1. Give everyone a sheet of paper and a pen or pencil. Ask group members to write ten words that describe themselves. It is very important that the words be nouns, not adjectives. Some examples are: *female, brother, mother, musician, Korean-American, athlete, dreamer, soprano* and *student*.
2. Allow about five minutes to complete this first part. Then ask everyone to narrow their list to five nouns, choosing the five they feel most strongly tell who they are. Students should write these nouns on the other side of the paper with a marker. These can be posted in the classroom to look at later if desired.
3. When everyone is finished, ask each group member to read his or her five nouns out loud. If the group isn't too large or if there is plenty of time, have the members explain why they choose some on their nouns.
4. When all sharing has taken place, discuss the following questions:

    - How many of the things listed would be visible to someone who was meeting you for the first time?
    - Were you surprised by any of the nouns?
    - What kinds of questions do we need to ask if we really want to get to know the real person?
    - What were some of your first impressions of the people in the group?
    - How have they changed?
    - How would knowing some of these self-interests add to the ability of the group members to get along?

That's Me!

Purpose: A quick and active way to discover the makeup of your group
Group Size: 15 or more
Time: 5 minutes
Supplies: None

Directions:

1. Arrange the group in a large circle. If you have more than 100 people, they can stay in their seats.
2. Tell the group that you will call out a variety of categories. If a person fits that category, he or she should run to the middle of the circle, shout "That's me!" and high-five any others who ran to the middle with them. Group members should do this for each category in which they fit. (If you have more than 100 people and limited space, just have them raise their hands and shout "That's me!")
3. Keep moving at a fast pace and have fun with this. It works well whether the students are moving or staying in their seats.
4. Use any categories you like, but here are some ideas. Adapt them for the age group.

- I am a senior (junior, sophomore, freshman).
- I am from (name of state, province, city, school).
- I am in student council.
- I am involved in sports.
- I am involved in drama or music.
- I like pizza.
- I have a big (small) family.
- I have a brother (sister).
- I am an only child (middle child, oldest, youngest).
- I was born in summer (winter, spring, fall).
- I have a job.
- I do volunteer work.
- I have a pet.
- My room is a mess (very clean).
- I can drive.
- I sing in a choir.
- I have been known to sing in the shower.
- I watch three or more hours of TV a day.
- I read at least one book in the last month.
- I play a musical instrument.
- I like to eat junk food.
- I like to eat healthy food.
- I love to laugh.

This Is Me

Purpose: A low-threat activity that gives people a chance to work closely with someone; can be done early in the formation of a group
Group Size: 10 to 30
Time: 15 minutes
Supplies: A copy of the This is Me Worksheet and a pencil for each group member

Directions:

1. Give each student a worksheet (page 66) and a pencil.
2. Instruct everyone to mingle and find a partner. Partners will now exchange worksheets and draw one feature of each other's face on the paper.
3. The artists sign their names in the spaces corresponding to the facial feature they drew.
4. Then each student should find another partner, exchange papers, and draw one facial feature for that person, who in turn draws one of his or hers.
5. Continue this until all students have their faces completely drawn.
6. Then have each student sign the back of his or her portrait and give it to you.
7. When all are seated again, hold up each picture. Ask the group to try and guess the person shown in the drawing. It's amazing how well some of the portraits turn out!

Twelve Squares

Purpose: To have students interact with and discover information about others in the group
Group Size: 10 to 25
Time: 30 minutes
Supplies: A Twelve Squares Worksheet (or blank paper) and a pen or pencil for each student

Directions:

1. Distribute the Twelve Squares Worksheets (page 67) or have each student fold a piece of paper into twelve squares.
2. To begin, have each person find a partner. Each person is to ask the other a question that will reveal a piece of information. Some typical questions are: How many people are in your family? What is the best book you ever read? Who is your favorite cartoon character? What kind of contest would you like to win?
3. Each person writes his or her partner's name and answer in a square. After both partners ask and answer a question, they move on to talk with someone else.
4. Students may pose the same or a different question to each person. If they use a different question for each square, they should keep track of which question was asked each time.
5. After everyone has filled up their squares, the group sits in a circle.
6. Ask "What did you learn about [Name]?" All who have talked with that person share their responses. The sharing should happen at a quick pace.
7. Continue until the group has heard about each member.

This is Me Worksheet

Who Drew This?

left eye _____   right eye _____

nose _____   mouth _____

neck _____   hair _____

left ear _____   right ear _____

left eyebrow _____   right eyebrow _____

Twelve Squares Worksheet

Two Truths and a Lie

Purpose: Reveals some information about each student; requires use of judgment skills; promotes discussion and always generates laughter

Group Size: 5 to 20

Time: 10 – 20 minutes

Supplies: 3" x 5" index card and a pen or pencil for each student

Directions:

1. Direct students to write their names and three facts about themselves on their index cards. Two of the facts should be true, and one should be a lie. Encourage the group to be creative.
2. Collect all of the index cards and mix them up.
3. Read each person's name and his or her three statements aloud.
4. Have students vote on which statement is the lie by holding up one, two or three fingers.
5. The votes don't really matter, but it is fun to see what everyone's guess is for the lie.

Uncommon Denominators

Purpose: Helps group members recognize that there are many differences among people and that those differences are valuable and necessary for working together and solving problems

Group Size: 6 or more

Time: 10 minutes plus sharing

Supplies: None

Directions:

1. Have group members pair up, and give them ten minutes to determine and discuss five things that they DO NOT have in common. They should do this by discussing attitudes, view points, experiences, etc. Stress that they should look for unique or important differences – things that tell the rest of the group something about "who you are" and "who you are not." (Unacceptable comparisons are things like different color of hair or eyes, styles of homes lived in or cars driven, etc.)
2. After ten minutes, have the entire group form a circle, and have the pairs share three (or all five, if time permits) of their differences.
3. Process the activity with the following questions:

    - What did you learn about the members of the group?
    - Why is it useful to understand differences?
    - When considering solving problems in your school, group or community, why might it be valuable to have differences?
    - What would be important to keep in mind in a group setting, knowing that there are many different viewpoints or experiences?
    - If you were forming a committee, would you invite someone with a differing view to join that committee? Why or why not?

Uniquely Me

Purpose: To think about and then share traits about oneself
Group Size: Unlimited
Supplies: Sheet of paper and a pen or pencil for each student

Directions:

1. Have each student trace one of his or her hands on a piece of paper.
2. In each finger (and thumb), list the following:

    a. something I'm proud of
    b. two of my good friends
    c. something I like about myself
    d. a person I want to be like and why
    e. what I most vividly see in my future

3. On the palm of the hand, have each student write two things he or she enjoys doing.
4. After everyone has finished writing, ask each person to share at least one response.

Up in the Air

Purpose: Provides a very lively activity that serves as a good springboard for discussion about juggling responsibilities in life
Group Size: 10 to 30
Time: 15 minutes
Supplies: One balloon for each person, plus 10 additional balloons

Directions:

1. Distribute one balloon to each person, and have everyone blow up their balloons.
2. Explain that the goal of the game is to keep all balloons in the air for as long as possible.
3. Point out that a penalty occurs when a balloon touches the floor, or if a balloon is left on the floor more than five seconds after it falls. You will call out a penalty as it happens. The group is disqualified after accruing five penalties.
4. Start the activity by saying, "Go."
5. Every ten seconds, add a balloon to those already in the air.
6. When the five penalties are reached, stop the activity, tell the group how long they kept the balloons in the air, and ask them to discuss how they could break their record. After a short discussion, have them try it again.
7. Process the activity.

    - What was your goal? Did you accomplish it?
    - Did you break your record with the second try? Why?
    - How did you feel when more balloons were being added to those already in the air?
    - Did you come up with a strategy to deal with the extras?
    - What are some responsibilities in your life?
    - What are some ways to juggle all of the responsibilities in your life?

Wacky Olympics

Purpose: A collection of activities done in teams; can be separate events or can run concurrently in one big event

Group Size: 10 to 25 per team

Time: Each game should be set for 3 - 5 minutes; a competition of ten games with up to ten teams takes about 45 minutes

Supplies: As listed for each game

Games

Alphabet Dancing – The team begins at the starting line. Three players run to a spot 15 feet away, lie on the floor and form the letter A with their bodies. All three people have to be part of the letter. After you approve of their formation, players run back to the starting line, and the next three people run down to the spot and make the letter B. Keep going through the alphabet (and start over if you have to) until time is up. Give one point for each letter made.

Balloon Pop – Arrange team members in pairs, and have them line up behind a starting line. Have a supply of deflated balloons about 20 feet away from the starting line (11-inch balloons work well). When you give the signal to start, the first pair must run to the balloons, blow one up, tie it, and then pop it. Once the balloon pops, they run back to the starting line, and the next pair goes. Give one point for each popped balloon.

Variation: Have only one person at a time run to the balloons, blow one up, tie it and pop it by sitting or stepping on it.

Basketball Bounce – Put a large garbage can or box about seven feet from the starting line, but don't have it tight against a wall. Each player takes a turn trying to bounce the basketball into the box or can. Players retrieve their own basketballs and bring them back to the starting line for the next player. Give one point for each ball that stays in the garbage can or box.

Bucket Pass – Have everyone lie on their backs in a circle, with heads toward the middle of the circle and feet in the air. Students must pass a five-quart ice cream bucket, a small box or a three-pound coffee can around the circle using only their feet. Give one point for each person who successfully passes the bucket. Continue until time is up.

Chariot Race – This time the team works in groups of three. Don't worry if it doesn't work out to be even groups – students match up as their turn comes. You need a strong blanket as the chariot. The object of the game is for one person to ride on the chariot (blanket), while the other two pull him or her to the finish line 15 feet away. At the line, one of the pullers hops on the chariot, the rider becomes a puller, and they pull the rider back to the start line. Keep this up until time is called. Give one point for each successful trip.

Cup Blow – Poke a hole in the bottom of a Styrofoam cup, and pass a five-foot long string through the hole. Attach the string to two chairs. The object is to blow the cup from one chair to the other. The person should be blowing into the cup, not onto the back side of the cup. Students will have to stoop or get down on their knees to be at cup level. Push the cup back to the starting spot when the blower gets it to the other chair. Give one point for each person who completes the task.

Frisbee® Toss – Make a two-foot by two-foot square on the wall with masking tape. Make a line on the floor with tape about ten feet away from the square. The object is to throw the Frisbee® so it hits the wall inside the square. Give one point for each hit in the square. (Experiment with the distance. You may have to adjust it for different age groups.)

Hula Hoop Relay – Have the group stand in a circle. Put a hula hoop over one person's arm, and then ask the whole team to hold hands. The object is to move the hula hoop from player to player without letting go of any hands. Count one point for each person who successfully passes the hoop. Continue until time limit is up.

Over and Under – Line up the team in a straight line, with everyone looking at the back of the head of the person in front of them. The first person is given a ball (a basketball, soccer ball or volleyball works well). The team's job is to pass the ball over their heads and between their legs in an alternating sequence. The first person passes the ball over his or her head; the second person passes the ball between his or her legs; the third person, over the head; the fourth person, between the legs; and so on. When the last person is reached, the ball is tossed up to the front person and they start again. This time the first person passes the ball between his or her legs, the second person passes the ball over his or her head, etc. Give one point for each person who handles the ball.

Plunger Run – Buy two plungers, take the head off one, and attach it to the end of the other plunger's stick (thus making a two-sided plunger). Arrange the team in pairs. The first two people position the plunger so that one end is on one person's belly and the other end is on the other person's belly. The pair must use their bodies to keep the plunger between them, and they can't touch the plunger. It works well if players put their hands on each other's shoulders. Pairs must run from the starting line, around a chair or cone 20 feet away, and then back to the starting line. Then the next pair runs the course. Give one point for each pair to cross the finish line.

Potato Squat – You need a few large potatoes and a low box for this game. At the starting line, the first player puts a potato between his or her knees. The player must hop/walk/ run to the box (about ten feet away) and drop the potato into the box. Once it falls in, the player should grab it out of the box and run back to the starting line. Then it is the next person's turn. Give one point for each potato dropped in the box.

Sponge Water Relay – The goal is to fill your team's bucket with more water than is in any other team's bucket. For each team you will need one sponge, a large five-gallon pail, at least one ice cream bucket, and something with which to measure the water. The first person on the team dips the sponge into the five-gallon pail, which is already filled with water. This person runs 15 feet to the ice cream bucket, squeezes out the sponge, runs back and passes the sponge to the next player. Measure the amount of water in each team's ice cream bucket after the time is up. The winner is the team with the most water. Be sure this game is only played outdoors.

Spooning – You need one spoon and a few cotton balls for this game. The object is to carry the cotton ball on the spoon from the starting line, around a chair about ten feet away, and back to the starting line. When the first person completes this loop, he or she hands the spoon off to the next person. Use very light cotton balls, as they are a bit harder to maneuver when one is traveling at top speed. Give one point for each successful trip.

Stepping Stones – The group works in pairs in this game. One person in the pair is given two paper plates. These are the stepping stones on which the other person has to cross the murky swamp. Player A sets down a paper plate, and Player B can put one foot on it. Player A then sets down the next plate, and Player B puts the other foot on it. Player A keeps alternating plates until Player B gets to the finish line, which is about ten feet away. Partners then trade places, so that Player B lays down the plates while Player A is the stepper. Give one point for each successful trip.

Straw Drop (or Clothes Pin Drop) – For this activity, you need about twenty straws and a container with a somewhat narrow neck. Taking turns, each person takes a straw, holds it to his or her forehead, and tries to drop the straw into the container. Each person then retrieves the straw from the container on the floor (or from the floor itself), and goes to the end of the line. Keep a count of the straws that make it into the container, and give one point for each straw. Substitute clothes pins for straws for a variation.

Tummy Tummy Ball – This is similar to *Plunger Run*. This time each pair puts a basketball between their tummies, runs around a cone that is set about 20 feet away, and then back to the starting line. Then the next pair runs the course. If the ball is dropped, the players can pick it up where they stopped and keep going. Give one point for each successful trip.

Wacky Javelin – For this game, you need one hula hoop and two or three foam pool noodles (Frisbees® can also be used). One of the team members is the hula hoop holder, who stands about ten feet from the starting line. The other team members take turns throwing the wacky javelin (a foam pool noodle) into the hoop. The hoop holder may move the hoop around to try to aid the javelin through it. You can also duct tape a small beanbag animal to the end of each javelin to help them fly better. Each thrower retrieves his or her javelin. Give one point for each time a javelin goes through the hoop.

Walk the Plank

Purpose: Calls for strategy and cooperation - or the alligators will eat you!
Group Size: 10 to 20
Time: 20 minutes
Supplies: Masking tape or a plank-like board

Directions:

1. If you are using tape, make a 10' by 14" rectangle on the floor. Adjust the length for the larger groups. This is the "plank."
2. Have the group line up on the plank in order of height (either shortest to tallest or vice versa). Their mission is to reverse the order of the lineup without stepping off the plank and into the alligator-infested waters. You may choose to time them to see how fast they can do this.
3. Check that no one steps out of bounds. If they do, declare them "eaten by the alligators" and out of the game – or just make the team go back to where they started.
4. It takes some time and teamwork to figure out the best solution to this activity. If you have more than one team, give an award for the fastest time, fewest people lost to the alligators, best teamwork even without the fastest time, etc.
5. Process the activity.

    - What strategy did you use to do this activity?
    - Did the group members change their minds many times?
    - Did anyone emerge as a leader?
    - What is the key to successfully completing this activity?
    - Where else in your life is it very important to cooperate?

The Wave

Purpose: Provides an activity for name introductions
Group Size: 15 to 100
Time: 5 minutes
Supplies: None

Directions:

1. Arrange everyone in a circle (either sitting or standing), and ask everyone to hold hands.
2. Have students find out the names of the people with whom they are holding hands.
3. Direct one group member (Tess, for example), to start the activity. Tess says the name of the person on her right, David, as they raise their hands together in the air. Then David says the name of the person on his right, Ben, and they raise their hands together. Ben says the name of the person on his right, and they raise their hands together. This pattern continues until it gets back to Tess.
4. Then reverse the flow by having Tess say the name of the person on her left.
5. See how fast the group can get The Wave to go around the group, first going counterclockwise and then going clockwise.

Web of Info

Purpose: Highlights how "connected" we can become with more information about one another
Group Size: 10 to 20
Time: 10 – 15 minutes
Supplies: Ball of yarn or string

Directions:

1. Have the group sit in a circle.
2. While holding a ball of yarn, ask and answer a question (see suggested questions below).
3. After answering the question, hold on to one end of the yarn, and toss the ball to another student.
4. That student answers the question, holds onto the unwinding strand of yarn, and tosses the rest of the ball to a new person. This process continues until everyone has answered the questions and is holding on to a piece of yarn, thus forming a spider web pattern.
5. Ask a new question and reverse the process. The person who ended up with the ball of yarn starts by answering the question, and then tosses the ball to the person holding the next piece of the yarn. That person rolls his or her strand of the yarn onto the ball, answers the question, and tosses the ball to the next person. This continues until the ball comes back to you, thus untangling the web.
6. Possible questions to ask:

    - What is your favorite time of day and why?
    - What do you think your role in this group will be?
    - What kind of store would you like to own and operate?
    - What project would you most like to carry out this year?
    - Who has influenced your life and why?
    - What is the nicest thing someone can do for another person?

What I Like about Me Is....

Purpose: Encourages group members to talk about themselves; gives each member a chance to share things that may not come out in a large group discussion
Group Size: 10 to 20
Time: 5 – 10 minutes
Supplies: None

Directions:

1. Have members pair up. One person of the pair is *A* and the other is *B*.
2. Have the Bs begin. For one minute, B should tell A, "What I like about me is…" Every sentence must begin with "What I like about me is…" There is no pausing allowed. An example would be: "What I like about me is that I help out when I am asked. What I like about me is that I like nature. What I like about me is that I like to laugh. What I like about me is that I'm nice to my brother."
3. After all As and Bs have finished, discuss with everyone about how it feels to talk about yourself (especially for a whole minute!).
4. Also, discuss what each partner learned about the other person.

What's Different?

Purpose: Tests everyone's powers of observation
Group Size: 6 or more
Time: 5 minutes
Supplies: None

Directions:

1. Have everyone find a partner and introduce themselves.
2. Give the partners thirty seconds to inspect one another, taking note of things about hair, clothing, jewelry, etc.
3. Have the partners turn back-to-back, and quickly change something about their appearances; for example, remove earrings, switch a nametag from one side to the other, or put a pencil in a shirt pocket.
4. Now, have the partners turn back around and see if they can spot what the other partner changed.
5. Repeat the activity with new partners.
6. Continue the activity until time is up.

What's in a Name?

Purpose: Helps students remember names; sets up a team-building atmosphere
Group Size: 10 to 50, divided into groups of 3 or 4
Time: 10 minutes
Supplies: Paper and pencil for each team

Directions:

1. Divide the group into teams of three or four people each (see *Getting into Groups* on pages 23-24 for suggestions). The teams must all have the same number of people, or one team will be at a disadvantage. If this is not possible, the team(s) with fewer people will use someone's middle name for the activity.
2. Give each team a paper and pencil, and have each team member write his or her first name on the top of the paper in block letters. If all but one team has four members, have the team of three use one person's first and middle name so that team will still have four names on the top of the paper.
3. Direct the teams to make as many words as they can out of the letters at the top of their papers. Allow seven minutes for this.
4. Recognize the team with the most words, as well as the team with the longest words (more than three or four letters).

When Someone Claps Twice...

Purpose: Provides an excellent exercise in working together; if anyone isn't paying attention, the result is a total breakdown in the activity

Group Size: 10 to 30

Time: 5 minutes plus discussion time

Supplies: Slips of paper with directions; one piece of candy per person

Directions:

1. Cut the page of directions (page 77) into individual slips. Give one slip to each person. There are 27 directions in this activity, and it is important that each student have at least one. If you have more than 27 people, you will need to create more directions and slips. If you have fewer than 27 people, you can give some people more than one slip.
2. Explain that everyone must work together to reach the goal. If everyone follows the direction on their slips, there will be a surprise at the end (see the last instruction).
3. Then clap twice to get the game going.
4. Watch the progression. Usually the activity will run through to the end smoothly. If it gets stopped somewhere in the middle, you have to decide if you want to try to keep the game moving along, or just let it stop where communication breaks down. Processing the activity is interesting whether the game is completed or gets bogged down.
5. When the activity is complete or stops because of lack of communication, take time to discuss it.

   - How did you feel as the activity went along?
   - What did you notice about group members during the activity?
   - What kinds of situations can you relate this to in everyday life?
   - If the activity didn't go to the end, how did you feel about not completing it? How did you feel if you didn't get to do your slip?
   - What aspects are important in setting and achieving goals?

When someone claps twice, stand up and say, "Good Morning!"

When someone says, "Good Morning!", get up and turn off the lights.

When someone turns off the lights, clap once and yell "It's dark in here!"

When someone yells, "It's dark in here!" get up and turn on the lights.

When someone turns on the lights, stand up and spin around twice.

When someone spins around twice, make a cow noise.

When someone makes a cow noise, stand up and say, "I'm glad to be here."

When someone says, "I'm glad to be here," WHISTLE.

When someone whistles, stand up and flap your arms like a bird.

When someone flaps his or her arms like a bird, stand on your chair.

When someone stands on a chair, say, "Get down from there."

When someone says, "Get down from there," make a loud sneezing sound.

When someone makes a loud sneezing sound, feel the forehead of the person next to you and shout, "Someone get a doctor!"

When someone shouts "Someone get a doctor!" sing *I'm a Little Teapot*.

When someone sings *I'm a Little Teapot*, walk around the group leader three times.

When someone walks around the group leader three times, laugh really loud.

When someone laughs really loud, stomp your feet.

When someone stomps his or her feet, do a cheerleading move or jump.

When someone does a cheerleading move or jump, tell us what time it is.

When someone tells us what time it is, shake hands and introduce yourself to the tallest person in the room.

When someone introduces themselves to the tallest person in the room, say, "I have a question."

When someone says, "I have a question," say "I have an answer."

When someone says "I have an answer," come to the front of the room and make the letter Y with your arms.

When someone makes the letter Y with his or her arms, come to the front of the room with two other people and make the letters M, C and A.

When some people make the letters M, C and A with their arms, hop on one foot for five seconds.

When someone hops on one foot, say "Here comes Peter Cottontail."

When someone says, "Here comes Peter Cottontail," give everyone a piece of candy.

Who's In Charge?

Purpose: Highlights imagination and cooperation
Group Size: 15 to 40
Time: 10 minutes
Supplies: None

Directions:

1. Have the group stand in a circle.
2. Ask one person to leave the room.
3. Tell the group to select someone to be in charge of the group. That person is to lead the group through various motions after the person outside the room returns. Some motions could be scratching the nose, winking, turning the head left or right, snapping fingers, kicking out feet, and so on. The leader can decide what motions to use, but he or she needs to change the motions frequently.
4. The group members need to follow the leader without giving away his or her identity. Explain that this will take a lot of strategy because it is hard not to look directly at the person in charge, which would give away the game very quickly.
5. The returning person stands in the center of the circle and tries to figure out who is leading the group.
6. After the first person names the correct leader, another person leaves the room, and a new person is selected to be in charge.
7. See which leader can stay in charge the longest.

Wink

Purpose: Provides a low-threat interaction game
Group Size: 15 to 50
Time: 15 minutes
Supplies: None

Directions:

1. Tell all players to close their eyes and hold out their thumbs behind their backs.
2. Explain that you will squeeze one of the extended thumbs to indicate that the person will be the "Winker."
3. When you say "ok," the players should open their eyes and walk around the room, shaking hands and smiling at others.
4. When someone is winked at, he or she must count silently to five, and then loudly and dramatically fall to the floor.
5. If a player thinks he or she knows who the "Winker" is, he or she can say, "I'd like to make an accusation. I think the Winker is _____."
6. If the player is right, the game ends and a new Winker is chosen. If the player is wrong, he or she must dramatically fall to the ground and is out of the game.
7. The game then continues as before until someone makes a correct accusation. It seldom gets all the way down to two people before someone makes the correct accusation.

Yes/No Line

Purpose: Looks at the values of group members; lets each person take a stand on a question or situation
Group Size: 5 to 30
Time: 30 minutes
Supplies: None

Directions:

1. Explain that you will present some situations, and each person will be given a chance to agree, disagree or stand somewhere in the middle on that issue. One side of the room will be the Yes/Agree side and the opposite side will be the No/Disagree side. Group members can stand anywhere along the imaginary line in between the two sides to indicate their positions.
2. Once members have taken a stand, ask some of them why they choose their positions on the line. Allow discussion on the issue.
3. The level of the statement or question should be appropriate for how well the group knows one another. Here are some ideas for starters:

   - It's ok to cheat on a test.
   - If I found a wallet with $50 in it and no identification, I would keep the money.
   - I owe my parents my best effort in all I do because they raised me.
   - A little white lie never hurts anyone.
   - The best way to get ahead in life is to go to college and get an education.
   - If something is bugging me about my friend, it's always best to tell him or her.
   - You've been working hard in class all year and a classmate wants to copy your notes. This person rarely pays attention in class. Do you let this person copy?
   - As a famous athlete, you are offered $2,000,000 to endorse a product you would never use. Do you endorse the product?
   - At lunch, your friends are criticizing another friend who isn't there. Do you speak up for this friend?
   - You get two really good seats on the bus hoping the attractive person you see will sit next to you. An old man asks for the seat first. Do you give it to him?
   - You've accepted a date when someone you'd much rather go out with calls and asks you out for the same night. Do you try to get out of the first date?

Yes - No - Blue - Black

Purpose: Gets people talking to one another
Group Size: Unlimited
Time: 10 minutes
Supplies: 5 tokens or counters for each person in the group (beans, pennies, or stones work well)

Directions:

1. Give each person five tokens to begin the game.
2. Tell everyone they must mingle and talk with other group members. They are to try to win as many tokens from the others as possible. Tokens are won by trying to get other people to say *yes, no, blue* or *black*. If someone says any of those words, that person must give a token to whomever they are talking. (The homonyms *know* and *blew* also count!)
3. If a person runs out of tokens, he or she can keep playing and try to win back some tokens but won't have any to give away until after winning some back.
4. The winner is the one with the most tokens after time is up.

Zip, Zap, Zoop

Purpose: Helps people relax and have fun with a fast-paced name-learning activity
Group Size: 15 to 40
Time: 10 minutes
Supplies: None

Directions:

1. Have everyone stand in a circle. Designate one person as *It* and have *It* stand in the center of the circle.
2. Instruct *It* to point to one person in the circle, say "Zip," "Zap" or "Zoop" to the person, and then count to ten out loud as fast as possible.
3. If "Zip" is said, the response must be the name of the person on the responder's right.
4. If "Zap" is said, the response must be the name of the person on the responder's left.
5. If "Zoop" is said, the responder must say his or her own name.
6. The person to whom *It* pointed must try to respond before *It* gets to ten. If *It* counts to ten before the responding person says the correct name, that person trades places with *It* and is in the middle.
7. If the responder says the correct name, then *It* continues and points to a new person.
8. Remind players to keep things moving – it makes for a much more exciting game!
9. The game continues for as long as you designate.